What a Modern Catholic Believes About

THE

CHURCH

by Andrew Greeley

the thomas more press
chicago illinois

ACKNOWLEDGMENTS

Excerpts from *The Church* by Hans Kung, © Verlag Herder KG Freiburg im Breisgau, 1967. English translation © Burns & Oates, Ltd. 1967, published in U.S. by Sheed & Ward, New York and used by special permission.

Excerpts from *This Church that I Love* by Yves Congar, O.P. New York: Dimension Books, 1969. Used by permission of the publisher.

Excerpts from "The Church and Mankind," *Concilium,* Vol. 1, No. 1, January, 1965. Used by special permission of the Paulist Press, New Jersey.

Excerpts from *The Church* (New Directions in Theology Today—Vol. IV), by Colin W. Williams. Copyright © MCMLXVIII, The Westminster Press. Used by permission.

Excerpt from "Reflections on Authority," *New American Review,* Vol. 8, 1970. Used by special permission of the author.

For Sue and Jardy Durburg

Contents

INTRODUCTION

I am not a theologian and this will not be a theology book, though I will, on occasion, lean on the theologians for support. I am a social scientist, an empiricist, and this will be an empirical book about the Church. I am not going to attempt to settle the issue of whether the local community is the fundamental unit in the Church though it does seem to me that the theologians who argue that it is have the upper hand in that discussion, but as a sociologist I will contend that the "essential experience of the church" that almost all of us have is the experience of the local community. The theologians may, if they wish, begin their description of the church with grand, sweeping theories about the church's structure, but as a social scientist, I wish to begin with the church where we all first experience it—at the level of the local parish community. I am suggesting that the seven-year-old is right when he responds to the question, "What is the Catholic Church?" by pointing to his parish church and saying its name. The second grader shows profound religious insight when he points at that church and says, "St. Praxides is the Catholic Church." If we did not have a vision blurred by theological controversies (which only recently began to recede into the past), we might see clearly enough to be able to say the same thing.

I shall not, therefore, devote much attention in this volume to those two critical issues of ecclesiastical theology of the last century and a half—primacy and fallibility. Nor will I address, until the end of the book, questions of ecclesiastical hierarchy and structure. It is not that I think that the papacy or the hierarchy are unimportant; quite the contrary. I will make a case at the end of the book that they are extremely important. I do not advocate less power for them but rather more power; however, I think that both papacy and hierarchy will acquire more power only through a drastic change in the way authority is exercised. And so, without at all denying the importance of the theological debates about papacy, primacy, infallibility and hierarchy, I would suggest that they are nonetheless, from the long-range view of the history of the Church, *relatively* important; in most Christian churches that the world has ever known, both papacy and hierarchy were not issues of fundamental importance.

Let us imagine a peasant parish in central France in the thirteenth century. The papacy was indeed a reality, but a distant reality, one that impinged relatively little on the life of the parishioners; and the hierarchy, save perhaps for the bishop of the diocese, was almost as distant as the papacy. What was present, and indeed overwhelmingly present, was the local Christian community. Similarly, until the late nineteenth century, the Church in the United States was relatively isolated from the papacy; Rome was weeks or even months—and on occasion years—away.[1] The bishop could readily be many days' distant from the community and, under normal circumstances, the only reality of the Church experienced by a Catholic was that of the local community.

Even today issues of primacy, infallibility, and hierarchy impinge on the lives of most Christians merely at the intellectual level. They have been taught in the catechism classes that these issues are important, and they even believe on intellectual grounds that they are in fact important; however, such questions have relatively little impact or relevance for the personal religious life of the Catholic. His contacts with the Pope are nonexistent (save perhaps for an audience in the massive basilica of St. Peter), and, with his bishop, minimal. Thus, he experiences his Church, if he experiences it at all, in the parish community.

I am not denying the intellectual importance of the issues raised by the questions of primacy, infallibility, and hierarchy. I am simply asserting that these issues are *relatively* unimportant in the daily experience of church for the ordinary Christian.

The emergence of a centralized worldwide papacy is a very recent phenomenon, and is the result of a peculiar combination of Cisalpine triumphalism in theology, the Renaissance style of curial organization, and modern means of transportation and communication. Detailed supervision of every aspect of the life of the American Church by the Pope through a functionary called the Apostolic Delegate became possible only with the development of the rapid ocean-going steamship and became truly effective only with the development of the transatlantic telephone and airplane. In other eras of the Church's history, even if technology had made such supervision and regulation possible, it would still have been resisted on the grounds that it was an abuse of authority. At one age in the Church's history, in fact, bishops who objected to such supervision might have appealed over the pope's head to a general council. There were even popes who argued that the council was superior to the papacy. Apparently, one conciliar document making such a claim was actually approved by a pope.[2]

The historical accident which combined modern communication and transportation with Cisalpine theology and Renaissance absolutism is an unfortunate one. The theology of triumphalism and the absolutist style of the Curia prevent the new worldwide papacy from having the power and influence it ought to have. Of all the popes who have sat on the throne of Peter since the transportation and communication revolution (roughly the twentieth century), only John XXIII seems to have understood the immense influence which the pope can command, and he exercised this influence precisely by ignoring triumphalist theology and by ducking around the centralized absolutism of the Curia.

The point of these remarks is not to try to take power away from the papacy; as I noted before, I want a more powerful papacy. The point is, rather, that one ought not to start from the papacy in considering the Church and especially not from the papacy as it presently operates—heavily influenced by historical circumstances, not at all typical of past situations in the Church.

I do not propose to address myself in this volume to the question of whether there ought to be "structures" in the Church. This may be a question which naive romanticists would like to discuss as an intellectual game but it has nothing to do with the reality of human relationships. Any human community will evolve some sort of systematic patterns of relationships. If we were to abolish all the "structures" in the Church today, then new ones would begin to develop tomorrow. At least two of the "structures" about which there is so much happy-talk among the naive romantics—the papacy and the hierarchy—are absolutely indispensable in some form for any religious faith which also purports to be a worldwide community. The pertinent questions are not whether we are to have structures but rather what shape the "structures" ought to take and what sort of mechanisms ought to be built into them to prevent them from ossifying. We can answer these questions only when we have a clearer idea of what the Church is. "Structures" exist to service the community and not vice versa and we do not, therefore, determine what the community is by discussing its structures; rather, we discover what the community is and then shape our "structures" to fit the nature of the community.

I propose first of all to investigate the Church as it manifests itself most forcefully in our lives—that is, as a local community. I then intend to turn first to the Scriptures and then the Second Vatican Council and its theological commentators to see how these sources can confirm and deepen our experience of the Church. Finally, I shall make some observations on how two of the "structures" of the Church—the leadership position and the priest-people relationship—might be modified in the years to come to facilitate the work of the local community of Christians.

NOTES

1. It took several years for Rome to confirm the appointment of John Carroll's first auxiliary bishop. As a matter of fact, by the time the appointment was confirmed the good man was dead. The problem was not Roman inefficiency but the slowness of mails from Europe to the United States and the risk of mail getting lost on a long and dangerous trip.

2. Anyone interested in pursuing this question at greater length is referred to "An Historical Note on the Constitution of the Church," Carl August Fink in *Concilium: Structures of the Church,* 1970, pp. 13–26. The relevant decree is the *Decree Frequens* from the Council of Constance. Apparently Pope Martin V approved the decree.

Chapter One
A TALE OF TWO PARISHES

The juridic-structural approach to the Church has been so much a part of our cognitive training that it is very difficult for us to put it aside temporarily and approach the Church from the other end; that is to say, the "end" of the grassroots community. If I am to be successful in leading the reader to begin to think about the Church from this perspective—a perspective which I argue is fundamentally much more important to him—I must first of all touch a responsive cord somewhere in his personality. I must find a way to release in him the complex assemblage of positive and negative feelings that he has experienced in the past about the local community that is his Church. When the reader and I are able to share some of the vivid emotions that we have experienced in our local communities, then we may be able to examine these emotions, and the reality which has occasioned such emotions.

I therefore propose to begin by describing the two parish communities that have meant the most to me in my own life—St. Ursula parish where I grew up and St. Praxides parish where I served for the first decade of my life in the priesthood. I cannot expect that the reader will have lived in parishes exactly like St. Ursula and St. Praxides, but if I am skillful enough in describing these two experiences which were so fantastically important to me, then the reader may begin to recall his own experiences of local communities. Then, we can talk about the Church.

St. Ursula was a Depression parish. Its streets were lined by tidy 1920 bungalows and two-flats. Its Irish parishioners (along with a handful of Italians) were solid, respectable members of the lower-middle class (spiced up by a few professionals and business executives like my father) but it was a time of economic stagnation and limited expectations. A job in hand was worth more than a college education. WPA had paved our streets but by the late 1930's most of the members of the parish were employed. They were not, however, so secure in their jobs that the purchase of a new radio was not a major expenditure. It was a parish of streetcars and buses. Many of us did not have cars and even those who did were disinclined to let their teenage children drive them. One went to school, to the show, the pool halls and the drugstores on foot, and if one was old enough to court, one frequently courted on long walks and on bus rides. It was a parish with a frame church which was eventually replaced by a gymnasium that served as a "temporary church" for almost two decades. It was a parish of street corners, of baseball in "prairies,"[1] and of touch football on the asphalt alongside our corner house. It was a parish of snowball fights with the "publics" during the wintertime and of basketball in back of garages in the summer. It was a parish of a kindly, gray-haired monsignor in failing health and of affable, wisecracking curates (and of one curate who had us reciting the dialogue Mass and belonging to organized Catholic action groups in the middle of the 1930's). It was a parish of nuns (all but one of our school teachers were nuns), some of whom were "nice" and others of whom were "crabs"—in about equal proportions as I remember. It was a parish of oppressive, dull religion books and of fascinating history and geography books, of "Palmer Method" prizes (though I never won one) and of Superiors who carried little hand bells that they compulsively sounded whenever faced with a crisis. It was a parish of carnivals and raffles, of novenas and missions (usually featuring incredibly bad sermons), of orderly "ranks" coming out of the parochial school, of crowded Sunday Masses with collection envelopes and sparse weekday Masses invariably said in black vestments. It was a parish where some of our more venturous teenagers enjoyed breaking up the camp meetings of our Protestant brothers (not brothers then) held in the summertime and of suspicious Greek ice-cream parlors where we were attracted by the vast scoops of whipped cream and frightened by the dark, swarthy males with (heaven forbid) long sideburns. (What we thought about the lovely Greek waitresses at these ice-cream parlors probably ought not to be here recorded.) It was a parish in which some of us, at least, looked up the Legion of Decency listing on a movie before we went to the "Manor" or the "Iris" and a parish where repeated attempts at collection drives to build our "new church" were greeted with complaint, dismay, and enthusiasm, though, in Depression years, rarely with success.

St. Ursula was a stable community, closed, loyal, warm —for many of us, the center of our lives. We were not then people of plenty; it was not an age of affluence. We were not inclined, most of us, to look beyond the religious or socioeconomic or educational borders of our parish. It was a gray-tinted world where we did not expect much and where both our anticipations and our disappointments were carefully controlled by the great and somber pall of the Depression.

Yet, for many of us the parish was the center of our lives (though we would hardly have thought of it, much less

described it, in those terms). If we were asked where we
were from we would not say Austin or Mayfield Avenue;
we would say St. Ursula. So much of our "identity"
(though we wouldn't have known the word then) was
Irish Catholic that our geography was expressed in Irish
Catholic terminology. It is important to emphasize, however, that we were not Irish Catholic consciously or explicitly; it was something we assumed, something that was
almost as pervasively a part of our lives as the air we
breathed.

Later I would come to understand the dynamics that
went into the construction of St. Ursula and I would know
that it was an "immigrant parish," though I am sure we
would not have thought of it as such in those days and the
implication that we were "immigrants" and thus something less than fully American would have been offensive
indeed.

I am gentle in my description of St. Ursula, perhaps
even nostalgic, though I liked it even in the 1930s and was
proud of it. Those of us who went off from it to the seminary were determined to sing its praises despite the taunts
about our basement church. There were immigrant parishes of the 1930s that gave one much less to be proud of
than did St. Ursula, and yet the criticism that one hears
from Catholic liberal intellectuals about the parish in
which they grew up frequently misses the point. The St.
Ursulas of the country were, indeed, narrow and, in the
fullest sense of the word, parochial. It's hard to see, given
the social and economic condition of the Catholic population of that time, how they could have been much else.
It's easy to be a social critic from the perspective of hind-
sight. If one evaluates St. Ursula from the perspective of
the 1970s it appears very inadequate. Its theology was un-
sophisticated to the point of being simplistic. Its liturgy

was generally meaningless ritual. Its worldview did not go beyond the boundaries of North Austin. Its style was autocratic with little flexibility and it was quite incapable of engaging in dialogue.

But it was not designed to do any of these things. It was designed, rather, to be the religious and therefore, inevitably, the social and human center of the life of as many of the children and grandchildren of the immigrants as sought such a center. To judge it by the standards of a post-immigrant and post-Vatican Church is to engage in a narrowness even worse than that of St. Ursula. Whether the post-Vatican local Christian community will achieve *its* goals nearly as well as St. Ursula achieved the goals of the 1930s still must be very problematic.

I was proud of St. Ursula in the 1930s and can understand it in the 1970s. The religious worldview with which it equipped me was incomplete but I am still grateful for that worldview because it gave me a place on which to stand. And although it may have been incomplete, it was at least openended; it is extraordinarily difficult to *go* somewhere unless one is *from* somewhere; and I'm from St. Ursula.

But if there is little ambivalence in my emotions about St. Ursula there is, and always will be, extremely strong ambivalence in my feelings about St. Praxides for it was a religious experience that remains in my bloodstream, I think to stay (if religious experiences can get into one's bloodstream). To say that it was the most important influence of my adult life is, if anything, to understate the case.

St. Praxides was another matter, quite different from St. Ursula. During the seven years I was in the seminary (1947–1954) a revolution occurred in the American Catholic population. We began to become members of the professional upper middle-class. St. Praxides was the fruit

of that revolution. The first day I drove down the broad
tree-lined streets of the parish, with its wide expanses of
neatly manicured lawns surrounding large and gracious
suburban homes, I knew I was in a different world from
St. Ursula. My first view of the almost finished parish
church, the first modern church in our diocese, confirmed
my hunch that I was involved in a whole new ball game.
I had been trained for a place like St. Ursula but I had
been sent to a parish whose existence had completely es-
caped our seminary faculty. Small wonder, for St. Praxides
represented the first large segment of the Catholic population of Chicago to make it into the ranks of the well-to-
do. I am not sure whether it represented the last flowering
of the immigrant Church or the first beginnings of the
post-immigrant Church, or perhaps both; but even though
my father was a business executive and, if he had lived, we
probably would have moved to some place like St. Praxides, neither I, nor indeed anyone, was prepared for a parish made up almost entirely of college graduates.

The well-to-do suburban parish is now well known in
American Catholicism; perhaps it is difficult to realize how
untypical it was in the early 1950s. When one's view of the
Church and the Church's mission in the United States has
been shaped by a mentality that is proud of the fact that
most of the faithful are "cap and seater people," one is
taken aback by country clubs and Cadillacs, by suburban
commuter trains, and real Notre Dame alumni instead of
the subway variety. When only two or three of one's grammar school classmates have gone to college, one is caught
off guard seven years later by a community where it is expected that all high school graduates will go through
college.

St. Praxides was the parish of the successful, well-edu-
cated business and professional men, their well-groomed,

handsome and frequently neurotic wives, and their baf-
fling, gifted, and frequently haunted children. I was
warned about those children during my first weeks in the
parish by everyone I talked to. The older priests, the nuns,
the adult lay people all told me that the grammar school
students and the teenagers were "spoiled rich kids" whose
parents had given them everything, who had no respect
for anybody or anything. In my decade there I searched
diligently for these spoiled young people but found only
one or two. All the others were, to a greater or lesser extent, intelligent, poised, respectful, and industrious. As a
matter of fact, they were so sophisticated that it took me
a long time to realize how much hollowness and self-re-
jection there was beneath the smooth veneer that they
presented to the world.

Those European sociologists who flocked to the United
States after the Second World War and were terribly upset
by the fact that the American Catholic population was still
going to church explained the high level of religious practice as a phenomenon of the national parish in the immigrant Church. Their confident prediction was that when
the immigrant parish broke up and the children and
grandchildren of the immigrants made it into the mainstream of American life, the levels of religious practice
would fall to where they were in France. St. Praxides,
then, was to be the place where the great drift away from
Catholicism should begin. My European colleagues could
not have been more wrong. Loyalty to the parish, enthusiasm over the Church—at least as it was perceived—generosity with time and money, commitment to every new
project that the parish sponsored (be it the Christian Family Movement or bridge marathons) in St. Praxides made
St. Ursula look quiet and stodgy by comparison. Instead of
drifting away from the faith and the loyalty of their par-

ents and grandparents, the third and fourth generation of Irish in St. Praxides had reached measures of religious behavior which I think have seldom been equaled in the long history of Christendom. Nor can the religious commitment of these well-to-do Catholic professionals be dismissed as mere culture religion, though surely it was very much a part of the culture of the neighborhood. It was a strange mixture of faith and boosterism, of tenacious clinging to the old combined with eagerness to find the new. We had the Sorrowful Mother novena and Cana conferences, the rosary during October and May, and the Gelineau psalms. Our pamphlet rack offered both *Our Sunday Visitor* and *Commonweal.* There were people in the parish who never got beyond *Extension* and others who read *Cross Currents* and the *New Republic.* Some of our teenagers were involved in Father Lawlor's decent dress and decent disk crusades while others had the opportunity to talk with Godfrey Diekmann, Daniel Berrigan (in an earlier manifestation), and George Higgins, and not a few managed to encompass both the Left and the Right with equal enthusiasm. It was a community terribly afraid, one might even say obsessed, with the thought of Negro "inmigration." Many of the people in the parish would rank high on any measure of social consciousness. And during the early 1960s, the era of John Kennedy and volunteerism, one authentically new lay movement (involving college students tutoring in the inner city) was born in St. Praxides.

St. Praxides had almost all that it takes—intelligence, enthusiasm, money, power, political and social leadership, and even, at least by the lights given it, religious commitment. Yet, there was something missing. It was not quite able to advance beyond the narrow bonds of suburban Irish respectability. This is not to say that there were not zealous and enthusiastic Christians at St. Praxides but it is to say that when the chips were down, when there were real opportunities either for individuals or for the community, one could never count on them. The community organization which, if it had worked, might have very well solved the problem of racial integration in the southwest side of Chicago, was torpedoed by suspicion and lethargy; and individual projects, especially among young people, would begin brilliantly, then gradually peter out usually resulting in bickering and inefficiency. Parents inevitably stepped in to raise two of the most terrifying questions which could be asked in St. Praxides: "What will people say?" and "Who do you think you are?"

The ultimate reasons for this paralysis at the last moment, when faced with an opportunity and a challenge which was both human and Christian, are beyond the scope of this book.[2] A dazzling, exciting, challenging, but ultimately depressing and discouraging place, the gloss of nostalgia does not blind me to the disappointments. I suppose it was foolish of one terribly energetic, but relatively naive young priest to think that he could turn St. Praxides around, to stir the South Side Irish out of their fear, their self-hatred, and their insidiously narrow respectability. I tried and I lost, and yet I must confess that if I had another chance I'd try all over again.

These, then, are my two basic experiences of church: a warm, stable, unexciting but supportive parish of childhood and a bedazzling, frustrating, obsessively fascinating parish of adulthood. The reader may not have quite as pleasant memories of his childhood parish nor quite so powerfully ambivalent feelings about the most important local church in his adult life, yet perhaps he begins to see what I mean. Both these experiences of church have precious little to do with infallibility, primacy, or any of the other arguments in the theology textbooks. They have very much to do with messy, complicated, primordial relationships which men and women fashion in that parish which is most meaningful in their life and in which they have invested the strongest commitments of their personality. Some will suggest that St. Praxides or St. Ursula were not *religious* in the sense that neither of them were "authentic, prophetic" communities, but this is a very narrow and *a priori* view of religion, a view which is quite isolated from the human condition. However, to the sociologist, a religious community is rather a group of people who share the same fundamental values about the most important things in their lives and gather together around this value system both to reinforce it by their unity and to share their lives with others whom they perceive to be, because of common values, "their kind of people."

In a previous volume[3] I pointed out that one of the principal functions of religion was to provide man with a set of answers to the fundamental questions he must ask himself about the nature of reality. The other basic function of religion is to provide man with something to belong to, a community of those who share with him, however imperfectly, the responses to these basic questions. The local church is that community of fellow believers who are part of the place where we eat and sleep, live and love, raise our children, grow old and die. It is generally a physical place though occasionally it can be a psychic one. But it is a place where we belong to other people and they belong to us.

The most basic thing, then, that can be said about the local church is that it is people, not perfect people, not saints, not angels free from the grip of social class, ethnic group, geography, or culture, but rather men and women caught not merely in the human condition but also caught in that particular segment of time and place which has shaped their culture and their personalities. The perfectionists are scandalized by this. It is shocking and disgraceful that a group which claims to be God's people should be so time-bound and place-bound, and they are quite correct. But there is no way that a faith community made up of human beings can escape the time and space of which it is a part. If the Church is made up of people then it is also necessarily composed of creatures who are limited and finite. Therefore, it follows that since the Church is made up of people, it will always labor under imperfection and inadequacy; or, as the scripture says, the bride will be without blemish only when the bridegroom returns. In some sense, one supposes, the Church is infallible, but the local community includes in its membership only weak and fallible human beings. This is a profound scandal to the perfectionists but our experience of Church tells us, if we are ready to examine that experience, that imperfection, weakness, fallibility, finitude are all part of the very nature of the Church, and will be eliminated only by eliminating people as its members.

Those of us who are used to beginning with a description of the Church that stresses its glories and its perfections are taken aback when someone starts his description of the Church with an insistence on the limitation which inevitably flows from the nature of its membership; and yet if we could reflect on our experience of Church and put aside the *a priori* dicta of the textbooks, the limitations and the imperfections of the Church look large in our experience. It is worth remembering that the Church described in the New Testament was also substantially less than perfect and that Jesus was quite explicit about his decision to bring his kingdom into being through the agency of the weak and the ignorant. When one looks around at the membership of the Church, be it either the members of the local community one knows best, or the leadership that one reads about, it is perfectly clear that the Lord's promise to work through the agency of the weak and the ignorant has not been violated. Of weakness and ignorance we do not have a shortage.

But one wonders whence comes the perfectionism. One hears from young enthusiasts today that if the Church does not eliminate all traces of "institutional racism," if it does not take an immediate stand for peace, then they will judge it to be "irrelevant" and leave it. Thirty years ago it was the cause of the trade unions that the Church was expected to dedicate itself to (a fact which would give the young enthusiasts pause if they ever bothered with such things as history). Again, we are told that the Church is irrelevant if it is not "poor" or "scientific" or "up-to-date" (which usually means rock music at Masses), or "committed to the Third World." In other words, the Church must be perfect now despite the fact that it has never been before, not even in the time of Jesus.

The call for the perfect Church is not new. It has been echoed by reformers down through history. Whether the reformers also became schismatics depended in great part on whether they insisted that the perfect Church be achieved instantaneously or whether they were willing to strive for it while awaiting fulfillment when the Lord returned. The sectarians who did break away found that the perfect Church they hoped to create soon suffered from all the imperfections of the old Church, but such a discovery did not prevent new generations of enthusiasts from rising up with the firm conviction that *they* could build the perfect Church.

The perfectionism of enthusiasts is even worse today. Knowing no history, raised in an atmosphere of triumphalism which led them to believe that the Catholic Church was virtually without flaw, they discovered to their horror that there was pettiness, inefficiency, venality, corruption, stupidity, ambition, greed, and hardness of heart within the Church. In other words, they discovered that it was made up of human beings who lived up to their own ideals very inadequately. To the youth of this and of every other generation such a discovery is unacceptable.

I do not, therefore, apologize for the fact that St. Ursula and St. Praxides were imperfect. I apologize for the imperfections themselves and for the fact that those of us who were part of both communities did not strive with more enthusiasm to eliminate, or at least curtail the imperfections. I certainly apologize that we became complacent with the gap between what we aspired to be and what we were. I decry the provincialism of St. Ursula and the racism of St. Praxides, but because they were imperfect and flawed I do not thereby deny them the title of church. Quite the contrary, I assert that such fallibility and imperfection are a necessary part of our experiences of church and that no one who has ever experienced church has ever experienced one which is anything more than fallible and imperfect.

The second thing that must be said about our experience of church in the St. Ursulas and the St. Praxides of our experience is that it is an experience with a definite sense of place, not merely physical place but also cultural and psychological place. (Some of the new, informal religious communities transcend neighborhood geographic boundaries but, if anything, their sense of psychological and cultural place is even stronger than that of the immigrant parishes.) In the 1930s or the 1950s in the Middle West, in the United States of America, among the children or the grandchildren of the Irish immigrants, our churches may have been committed in theory, and occasionally in practice, to a universal affiliation but, like their members, we were very much a part of a segment of time and a piece of space. The universal idealism that we professed was necessarily incarnate in our geography and culture; indeed, so complete was the incarnation that we too rarely felt the tension between the universal and the particular that ought to have existed. The parishes were very like their members, limited by the cultural, physical, and psychological environments in which they found themselves.

Those parishes, however, were still relevant to their people and their peoples' problems. In fact, by its very definition, any religious community which holds its members is relevant to the needs of its members. Those enthusiastic critics who decry the "irrelevance" of the Church mean in fact that the Church does not respond to the critics' needs, or to what the critics perceive *ought* to be the needs of the membership. But St. Ursula was extremely pertinent to the problems and difficulties of the children of the immigrants during the Depression and St. Praxides was equally pertinent to the needs of the new rich in the 1950s. To maintain one's faith, one's tradition, one's identity while trying to "make it" in a new nation is a fundamental human need, and the success of St. Ursula and St. Praxides was rooted in their capacity to respond to this need. Enthusiasts, of course, reject the right of the new rich or the immigrant to have such needs: Consequently, a Church which is incarnated in time and space as occupied by these two groups is necessarily seen not merely as an imperfect Church (which of course it is), not merely as an irrelevant Church (irrelevant to them, that is), but also as a false Church. The only Church which would be a true one would be one which would devote its principal energies to denouncing the immigrants for their provincialism and the new rich for their insecurities.

Obviously, a Church—at least a Christian one—should strive to break out of the boundaries of its segment of time and place (and I hope to make that clear later in the book), but I'm arguing against the perfectionists and the enthusiasts that a Church can move beyond its own geographic and cultural limitations only by recognizing that it is located in time and space and not by attempting to deny its location. Whatever we priests of St. Praxides accomplished during the 1950s and the 1960s was a result not of denouncing the new rich because they were new rich or by ridiculing their religious needs, but by understanding them *where they were* and trying to move beyond that. For the young enthusiasts, of course, such respect for the location of people (unless, in the current milieu, they are black or young) is intolerable.

Thirdly, the St. Ursula and the St. Praxides of the land had their leaders, men who symbolized by their person and their position the loyalties and aspirations of their parishioners. I'm not saying that these men were necessarily liked by their people (though in the two parishes I knew they were; as a matter of fact, the last pastor I knew at St. Ursula was a man of consummate political skills, and if he had chosen a career in government instead of church he could easily have been a ward committeeman or perhaps a mayor). What I'm saying, rather, is that even those who did not like the leaders acknowledged them, however reluctantly, as leaders, as the men who, incarnating the values and goals of the community, were expected to direct the community towards the achievement of those goals. They may have been autocrats—though in the two parishes I knew the autocracy was of an indirect variety—but even their autocracy provided the focus around which the community could rally. Our experience of church seems always to involve a man—or a group of men, or a group of men and women—whose responsibility it is to speak for and to the community. They interpret both the religious condition and the present situation in terms which the rank and file find more or less responsive to their own perceived needs. The legendary tyrannical Irish pastor was able to maintain the consent of his parishioners not so much because they held him in superstitious fear but because his leadership role was perceived as essential to the community. You might have preferred to have a more kindly and progressive pastor, but you knew you had to have a pastor. The alternative to a pastor was chaos; and for both the immigrant and the new rich, chaos in their religious community was unthinkable.

There has been a good deal of ink spilled about the tyrannical, reactionary Catholic pastor. I am not sure that he was any worse than the tyrannical neurotics who frequently seem to dominate our new post-Conciliar parish councils. I personally find both varieties of men insufferable but it seems to me that the former, even at his worst, would respond to certain authentic human needs; the latter responds to nothing but his own neurosis. But the point in our attempt to discover the meaning of our experience of church is not that some pastors were tyrants, not that the pastor, curate, and rectory-parish relationships were structured by an outmoded canonical juridicism. The point is, rather, that no one has ever experienced a church where there is no leadership; those churches which presently try to operate without leadership—either *de facto* or *de jure*—will not be church for very long.

We also experienced the sacred in our church. Mass in the basement church in the 1930s was not, I fear, a very artistic liturgical experience. Much of the time most of us didn't know what was going on. The Sorrowful Mother novena and benediction were more intelligible to us than Mass, and first Friday devotions were infinitely more popular than our first tentative attempts at the dialogue Mass. At St. Praxides there was a modern, beautiful church, Mass of the day, more developed forms of liturgical participation, and as many as half the parishioners at daily Mass during Lent. It was an artistic devotional improvement over St. Ursula but, by the standards of the liturgical movement, quite inadequate.

In both parishes the Mass did symbolize the parish, however obscure a symbol it may have been. The church where Mass was celebrated was the center of the parish (along with the school of course). It was to the church where we came for baptism, marriage, first Mass, and death. It was in the church that our children graduated from school. It was to the church that we scurried to acknowledge our sinfulness. It was in the church with downcast eyes that we walked reverently to the altar to receive holy communion. However imperfectly we understood these symbols, and indeed however theologically inaccurate our interpretation may have been, they were still important symbols in our lives because they said we were Catholics, and we were part of this parish, and these two identifications were deeply meaningful to us. Even though our devotion may have been privatist in the extreme it still took place in a public context. We went to church to see and be seen. This did not mean that our devotion was "merely" social but it does mean that it was deeply imbedded in relationships that constituted our lives. Just as the pastor was the man who symbolized the needs and the goals of the community, so "going to church" was a symbol of our own commitment to those goals. Perfectionists will argue, of course, that the symbols were poor symbols and the goals were limited goals. One can only respond that all human symbols are poor symbols and that all goals are limited goals. The perfectionist will then say that both the symbols and goals were not as good as they might have been, and all we can do is nod our head wearily, and agree that they weren't. Whether he has any better ones for our era remains to be seen. The point is that the sacred as we experienced it at St. Ursula and St. Praxides and the other churches like them was a sacred that did have some meaning, however limited, however transitory, in our lives.

Loyalty was something very much a part of our experience of church. We were proud of our parishes and while we might complain about them among ourselves we would be inclined to defend them fiercely against outside critics. We invested a good deal of ourselves in our church financially, of course, but also humanly. The church was figuratively as well as literally close to where we lived. Our parish was part of our identity. The parish church was where we came into contact with the sacred. Our parish school was where we were confident our religious tradition would be passed on to our children. The priests and the sisters were our religious leaders, however critical we may have been of them at the time. Our fellow parishioners were those who were banded together with us to preserve our particular values against the values of an outside culture which to the immigrant parish seemed threatening and to the new rich parish seemed ambiguous.

In the late 1940s some of us began to read the writings of the French Abbe Michonneau in which that worthy French ecclesiastic described the splendid new techniques being used in France to create a sense of community among members of urban parishes. Many of us lamented the fact that Abbe Michonneau's techniques were not being used in American parishes—although if they had been transferred without modification from France to the United States it is certain that most American Catholics would have been completely befuddled by them. But others of us perceived that what Abbe Michonneau and his brave colleagues were trying to create we already had. Oh, our sense of community and of loyalty to the community may have been inadequate and imperfect, it may have been flawed by all sorts of human frailties, but if it was loyalty to a religious community you were looking for we had it at Ninety-third and Hoyne in 1958 in an intensity which I daresay would be hard to match anywhere in the world.

We were loyal to our church because we cared about it. Some of us cared more about it than others. For some of us it was one of the most important realities in our life, while for others it was a reality that took on importance only on special occasions. But even those who left it could not leave it alone for, as love for the parish turned into hatred, it was usually a passionate hatred. One need only read James T. Farrell's devastating description of "St. Patrick's" in his Studs Lonigan trilogy to realize how important that church at Sixtieth and Michigan was to him during his childhood and adolescent years. Some of those critics of the parish who have adopted a pose of alienation cannot understand our romantic attachment to our old parishes but such alienated critics never really experienced the pervasive atmosphere of such a church (or if they did experience it, they identified it completely with parent figures from whom it was necessary to become alienated). Local churches were very much like women, some of them more attractive than others, but all are attractive, and on certain occasions anyone can become extraordinarily attractive. The parish was *there;* it was so *present* in our lives that strong emotions towards it, either love or hate or a combination of both were inevitable. I know that I will never get over my love affairs with St. Ursula and St. Praxides and I am sure that many of my readers have had similar intense experiences with their parochial communities. However imperfect and flawed these experiences may be from the point of view of prophetic religious purity, they are still, I would argue, very much part of the essence of church.

But at the root of all these other characteristics of the church we experienced is one that I think is the most essential. Our church was a quest for unity, a quest that was ultimately unsuccessful, but one which was still primordial and fundamental in our lives. One of the most basic of human experiences is the experience of separation. The child comes into the world loudly protesting the unfairness of being separated from his mother's body. He protests with equal vigor and perhaps more pain when he discovers that he is psychologically separated from his parents, that he must struggle against them and that ultimately he must bend his own ego to the demands of theirs. Our whole life is a quest to reestablish unity with other human beings, with the physical world, and even with ourselves. Marriage, friendship, contemplation, ecstasy, all these are manifestations of man's primordial quest for union. The church or the religious community is one of our more important attempts to achieve unity with our fellows. Precisely because it is a unity based on supposedly common assumptions about the ultimate nature of reality, we argue, implicitly at least, that it ought to be easy to love those who stand for the same things that we do, who have the same symbolic leader we do, and who participate in the same sacred ceremonies we do. The small-group religious communities of the present are a conscious, explicit, and very intense quest for a unity which will stitch together fragments of our human experience; but the immigrant parish and the new-rich parish were also a quest for unity, though explicit and less intense. In the agonies of adjusting to the new world we came together to strengthen our resolve not to give up our traditions. We came together to cope with the complex social and emotional and religious problems that arose when we plunged into the mainstream of American life. Our quest for unity was flawed (as it is, incidentally, frequently flawed in the small group church). Feuds, factions, rivalries, tensions, animosities erected huge barriers to our unity, but they were barriers of fear set up to protect us against the very powerful demand that the church as a social system made upon us. We used to lament in St. Ursula and even more in St. Praxides that the parish was like a small town, that there was no privacy, that we lived in a goldfish bowl, and that everyone knew what everyone else was doing; but such a sense of being "exposed" to others, of losing one's privacy is inevitable in any intense human relationship. While the churches we experienced in the past were not nearly so intense as a marriage relationship or the small-group communities of the present, they still provided powerful social support for the children and the grand-children of the immigrants. If we often felt ambivalent about the power the parish had over us, it was because powerful social support inevitably brings with it powerful social control—as the Communards found out, frequently to their dismay.

Both the thrust towards unity and the ambivalence about the unity are essential not merely to our experience of church but to all human experience of religious community. The religious community, whether it be among the Pigmy in the rain forests of Africa, the Israelites wandering in the Sinai desert, the Franciscans in the lanes to Umbria, or the underground church in the faculty members' dining room on a university campus, are all attempts to use common conviction about the fundamental nature

of reality as a basis for breaking through the barriers that
isolate us from our fellow men. The quest for unity may
be implicit or explicit, intense or very mild, but it's always
there whenever men and women come together with
"their own kind of people" to set up a community of fellow
believers.

If we examine our experience of church as we felt it in
the churches to which we have belonged, we discover that
it is an imperfect and flawed but very human community
rooted in a specific segment of time and space, grouped
around a leader who symbolizes its needs and goals. A
church engages in sacred actions that ratifies its existence,
demands loyalty and affection, and represents a strong
thrust in breaking through barriers of distrust, suspicion,
and alienation towards the formation of some kind of
unity. Some members of the church may be on the fringes,
others may be at the core; some may feel strongly, others
may have only slight emotional involvement. Some parishes may be effective in their quest for unity, others less
so; some may be intelligently led, others not; some may
never get beyond their own time and space, others may
lead at least a handful of their members to an understanding of the more universal dimensions of religious commitment. But the experience of religious community always
involves human beings in time and space groping towards
unity with one another as they gather around a leader and
celebrate the sacred.

Obviously, St. Ursula and St. Praxides have no monopoly on such religious community; indeed, the Roman
Catholic parish or the Christian congregation have no
monopoly on such a definition of religious community.
What is unique to our experience is a set of convictions,
however inadequately and imperfectly perceived, around
which a community is organized. What is unique to us is

the message and person of Jesus. Or to put the matter the other way around: From the point of view of the man of faith, Jesus did not come to abolish the human quest for religious community but to provide the most powerful cement for holding together the web of relationships that constitute the community—himself and his gospel.

The perfectionist eagerly points out that the person and the gospel of Jesus were understood very imperfectly both at St. Ursula and at St. Praxides. I must, of course, agree with him, but I would add that the message and person of Jesus have never been understood adequately. We could have done a much better job of preaching him or believing him in those two parishes. And yet preach him, however poorly, we did; and believe him, however weakly and inadequately, we did. That made us Christians—poor, weak, inadequate, fallible Christians; Christians in need of vast improvement, Christians inexcusably negligent in our response to the gospel, very sinful Christians. Yes, indeed, we were all of those things, and it is simply another way of saying that we were the people for whom he came to bring life.

NOTES

1. A term which Chicagoans of our generation used to describe vacant lots.

2. For anybody interested in pursuing the question further, he is referred to my article *"The American Irish Since the Death of Studs Lonigan"* in the *Critic*, May-June, 1971.

3. *What A Modern Catholic Believes About God* (Chicago: Thomas More Press, 1971).

Chapter Two

THE CHURCH AND GOD'S KINGDOM

We have established that the Church we experience is a community of human beings seeking unity with one another. Their quest for unity is based on their common conviction about the nature of reality; and that conviction in its turn is a commitment to the message and person of Jesus of Nazareth. The Church is a network of human beings trying to find unity by responding to Jesus. If we are to understand the Church, then, it is necessary to understand the message of Jesus. We must turn to sacred scripture to determine what the message of Jesus was. Much of the amateur "pop theology" appearing in the Catholic Church today would view this as a vain exercise, for it is assumed by all too many Catholics (including priests and nuns) either that scripture is irrelevant or that "scripture studies" have revealed that it is impossible for us to know what the message of Jesus really was. One must observe that those pop theologians who are convinced of this have not bothered to read the books of such scholars as J. Jeremias, G. Bornkamm, R. H. Fuller, N. Perrin, and E. Käsemann. Hans Küng summarizes the real state of New Testament studies at the present time:

It is of course far from easy to gather the original message

of Jesus himself from the source available. The gospels
are not neutral historical chronicles, but committed and
committing testimonies of faith. They are not written from
the perspective of Jesus before his resurrection, but from
that of the Church after his resurrection. And yet these
testimonies of faith also include reports of Jesus and his
message. The background to the gospels, and in particular
the first three synoptic gospels, is not legend and specula-
tion, but living experiences and impressions, reports
handed down about the living Jesus of Nazareth. If not
directly, at least through the evangelists' testimonies of
faith we can hear Jesus himself speaking. Anyone who
comes to these documents with essential rather than pe-
ripheral questions and puts them seriously rather than
casually, will receive answers which are remarkably clear,
consistent and original; answers which are obviously not
just the product of a chance coincidence of various theological versions of the truth, but which—however much
occasional details may seem historically dubious—speak
to us with the original words of Jesus.[1]

The first observation that must be made about the
teaching of Jesus is that he rarely mentions the word
"church." Indeed, it occurs in only two passages in St.
Matthew's gospel. (Concerning these passages, incidentally, the exegetes are engaged in violent controversy:
Matthew 16:18 and 18:17.) As a matter of fact, most contemporary scripture scholars argue that Jesus did not begin a formal organization during his pre-Easter ministry
comparable, for example, to the monastic community
which existed by the shores of the Dead Sea. Jesus was
not interested in setting up a sect like the Pharisees or the
Essenes. According to the exegetes, if he had been seen as
the founder of a separate synagogue, a new exclusivist
community, the fundamental theme of his message would
have been obscured and confused. In his pre-Easter period
Jesus laid the foundations for the church that would

emerge after his resurrection both by what he said and did. W. G. Kümmel, as quoted by Hans Küng, summarizes this point neatly.

There can be no question that Jesus reckoned upon his disciples gathering together again after his death and resurrection and sharing in a common meal and that, waiting and persecuted, they would be opposed by the great mass of the unbelieving members of the ancient people of God. The common experience of personal communion with the living Jesus, especially as a result of communal meals, would inevitably have led, in addition to the common experience of the resurrection, to a new alliance between the disciples. It was their common allegiance to Jesus, to the "man" now hidden, but who would soon reveal himself in glory, which according to Jesus' expectation would remain a constant factor for the disciples, even after his death, and would continue to bind them together. The fact that Jesus would then no longer be among them as an earthly human being, but that they could believe that through his resurrection he had already entered into God's glory, would not only strengthen them in their waiting for the parousia, but also in their certainty that the coming eschaton had already irrupted into the present in the person of Jesus.[2]

What then was the message of Jesus, which a sectarian community would have blurred but which would bind together his followers after his resurrection in a totally new kind of human community? It was first of all a message of a kingdom; the Greek word _basileia_ appears more than one hundred times in the first three gospels. Hans Küng quotes the words of Alfred Loisy, "Jesus proclaimed the kingdom of God, and what came was the Church," and notes that Loisy was not being ironic or snide. It would be a mistake to equate the Church with the kingdom, but one can certainly say that the Church is the response of those who believe in the kingdom.[3]

God's kingdom in the preaching of Jesus is not his universal lordship over his creation but is rather a decisive intervention of God in the course of human affairs. It is an "eschatological event which," in the words of Rudolf Bultmann "[would] destroy the present course of the world, wipe out all the contradivine power under which the present world groans and thereby terminate all pain and sorrow, bringing salvation for the people of God which await the fulfillment of the prophet's promises." Jesus, in other words, was preaching that the Really Real was in the process of inserting itself in human affairs in a radical and dramatic way.

God's intervention was seen not as something that could be earned by men or could be controlled by them but something that was a pure gift, totally on God's initiative. Furthermore, and here Jesus was quite insistent, it was not a political kingdom but rather a strictly religious one. Even though he was accused by his enemies of being a religio-political zealot, Jesus in fact refused to become involved in politics. The attempts of the politically minded of the Right or the Left to identify their cause with Jesus or his church find no confirmation in the gospel stories.[4] The kingdom that Jesus preached was not a kingdom which threatened disaster or punishment. Jesus did not come in order to bear witness to God's anger but to bear witness to his mercy. He came to the poor, the oppressed, the downtrodden, the sinners, and the godless. The kingdom is a saving event for sinners, not just a justification for those who are firmly persuaded of their own righteousness.

Furthermore, the kingdom of God is a call to repentance, a *metanoia*. This does not mean that one merely gives up certain habits. The *metanoia* Jesus demands is a total transformation of one's life which is manifested in a radical decision for God, a radical response of trust and belief in God's loving and saving intervention. Professor Joachim Jeremias in his masterful book, *The Parables of Jesus*, argues persuasively that most of Jesus' parables are challenges demanding that his hearers respond to him and his message. In the concluding paragraph of his book, Jeremias says:

> In attempting to recover the original significance of the parables, one thing above all becomes evident: it is that all the parables of Jesus compel his hearers to come to a decision about his person and mission. For they are all full of "the secret of the Kingdom of God" (Mark 4:11), that is to say, the recognition of "an eschatology that is in the process of realization." The hour of fulfillment is come, that is the urgent note that sounds through them all. The strong man is disarmed, the forces of evil are in retreat, the physician has come to the sick, the lepers are cleansed, the heavy burden of guilt is removed, the lost sheep has been brought home, the door of the Father's House stands open, the poor and the beggars are summoned to the banquet, a master whose grace is undeserved pays his wages in full, a great joy fills all hearts. God's acceptable year has come. For he has been manifested whose veiled kingliness shines through every word and through every parable—the Saviour.[5]

But there is something appallingly simple about this message of Jesus: God loves us, God is intervening, God is forgiving and saving. God wants our response. We ask, "Is that all it's about? Do all the theology books, all the papal encyclicals, all the decrees of general councils, all the debate, all the answers we've memorized—do they all come down to that brief and simple message?"

The only answer is, "Yes."

But the point is not that the message is so simple to state and so easy to understand. The point is rather that the response is so difficult. To really believe in God's loving intervention and to commit ourselves in trust to him requires far greater faith and courage than most of us have ever been able to display. God's power is at hand and we are not quite sure whether we are willing to trust it. That is the fundamental dilemma that has plagued the Christian church from the very beginning.

Finally, the sign of God's kingdom is that those who respond to it dedicate themselves to lives of love and service. In the concluding chapters of St. Mark's gospel, it is repeatedly demanded of Jesus that he work a sign to validate his message. Two kinds of signs would have been appropriate: either an apocalyptic wonder in the sky (like putting the sun out of business for a few days) or, even better, a military-political sign. If Jesus could have arranged to defeat the Roman armies his audiences would have been satisfied. But Jesus resolutely refused to produce any sign. He insisted that the Son of Man would be the sign of the Suffering Servant, that the presence of the kingdom he had come to preach would be known by the generosity and enthusiasm with which his followers gave themselves over to the loving service of others. The words of St. John's account of the Last Supper discourse summarized it neatly: "By this shall all men know that you are my disciples, that you have love for one another."

The Sermon on the Mount is another manifestation of what life is like in the kingdom of God. Professor Jeremias, in his splendid little booklet, *The Sermon on the Mount,* points out that neither the older Catholic nor the older Protestant interpretations of the sermon are valid. The Catholic position was that it presented the more perfect ethical ideal that men were invited but not obligated to follow. The Protestant position, on the other hand, was that the Sermon on the Mount represented the strict ethical demand that Jesus was imposing on his followers. We are of course incapable of living up to this demand, but Jesus in his mercy obtains forgiveness for our failures.

What Jesus really said was that those who truly believe in him and truly trust in him and truly give themselves over with enthusiasm to God's kingdom are able to live in such a way that their lives are a sign that God's kingdom is at hand. "In your lives rooted and grounded in the *basileia*, the kingdom of God, the victory of the kingdom of God should be visible."[6] The lives of those who accept the kingdom are as the light on the mountaintop to which all men are attracted. Jeremias concludes his pamphlet with these words:

> The sayings of Jesus which have been collected in the Sermon on the Mount are not intended to lay a legal yoke upon Jesus' disciples; neither in the sense that they say: "You must do all of this, in order that you may be blessed" (perfectionist conception); nor in the sense: "You ought actually to have done all of this, see what poor creatures you are" (theory of the impossible ideal); nor in the sense: "Now pull yourself together, the final victory is at hand" (interim-ethic). Rather, these sayings of Jesus delineate the lived faith. They say: You are forgiven; you are the child of God; you belong to his kingdom. The sun of righteousness has risen over your life. You no longer belong to yourself; rather, you belong to the city of God, the light of which shines in the darkness. Now you may also experience it: out of the thankfulness of a redeemed child of God a new life is growing. That is the meaning of the Sermon on the Mount.[7]

So the fundamental message of Jesus is that of the kingdom, which represents the decisive, gratuitous, crucial, challenging intervention of God in human history. This intervention is religious rather than political and demands of us who hear it a decisive total response of faith and trust, a response which in its turn is evidenced by a life of loving and generous service. It is this message and our response to it that represents the rationale of the church. The church is the community of those who respond more or less enthusiastically, more or less completely, more or less adequately to the Good News of Jesus. The church is, of course, a community of sinners, because it is precisely for sinners that Jesus came. It does not claim to be composed of saints; indeed, its claim to holiness is based rather on the fact that Jesus and the heavenly Father overcame the sinfulness of the members of the church, just as its claim to infallibility in the final analysis must mean that the horrendous mistakes that the members of the church and their leaders have made down through the ages are neither strong enough nor disastrous enough to stave off the results of God's merciful and loving intervention or to prevent the coming of His kingdom.

The real challenge to us is whether we believe in the kingdom. Do we believe that God does intervene decisively in human events? Are we ready to commit ourselves in total trust and faith to that intervention? Those who dismiss as pious legend this message of loving intervention can make no claims to be Christian. But most of us are far more clever than that: we do not say "no" to Jesus' challenge, we say "yes, but. . . ."

We will not devote much attention in this book to the question of whether Jesus believed either that God's kingdom had already come and that he was preaching its arrival or that it was yet to come at some unspecified date in the future. After more than a half century of debate on this subject, the common consensus of most exegetes is that both themes were involved; that Jesus saw the kingdom both as present and as yet to come. He saw himself preaching in a time between the "already" and the "not yet." It is also safe to say that the majority of exegetes are now persuaded that Jesus did not commit himself to a specific time for the fulfillment of the kingdom. The important point for him was not when the kingdom would be fulfilled but that men decide in favor of it. His sense of urgency was rooted in the fundamental importance of the message. In Hans Küng's words:

> . . . the decisive element of Jesus' message lies not in the expectation of an imminent end, but in the challenge to decide here and now for the reign of God. But in rejecting the expectation of an imminent end . . . we should not reject any kind of expectation. The fact that the expectations of an imminent end were not fulfilled should not lead us, like the mockers of II Peter 2:3, to conclude that any expectations of something in the future are misplaced. If we stress the presentist character of the reign of God and the importance of a decision which always has to be made here and now, must we then conclude that the whole future of the reign of God must be dissolved into the present? Does the "now" of an already fulfilled reign of God exclude a future "then," a reign of God which God himself will complete in the future? Jesus himself does not resolve the tensions between presentist and futurist eschatologies, neither by reducing presentist eschatology to futurist eschatology, like the apocalyptics of his time, nor seeing futurist eschatology exclusively in terms of presentist eschatology. . . .[8] pg 62 93

The church, then, is the assembly of those who responded more or less well to the challenge of the kingdom that Jesus preached. It is that group of men who live between the kingdom already begun and the kingdom not yet fulfilled.

The church (*ekklesia*), however, is not to be totally identified with the kingdom. The words of Küng are excellent on the subject:

> *Ekklesia* is a pilgrimage through the interim period of the last days, something provisional; *basileia* is the final glory at the end of all time, something definitive. *Ekklesia* em-

braces sinners and righteous, *basileia* is the kingdom of the righteous, of the saints. *Ekklesia* grows from below, can be organized, is the product of development and progress and dialectic, in short is definitely the work of man; *basileia* comes from above, is an unprepared action, an incalculable event, in short is definitely the work of God. God is the subject of this reign, he himself as the Lord and Father acting in kingly freedom and sovereignty. The reign of God is *his* kingly dignity, his act and his domain.[9]

But if the church does not represent the total fulfillment that the kingdom does, nevertheless it is intimately associated with the kingdom. It is a pilgrimage towards the kingdom; it is a sign of the coming of the kingdom. It is the herald and the voice announcing that the kingdom is at hand. The church is the community of those who believe in the kingdom, who preach the kingdom, who wait for it, and whose lives are a sign of its love and splendor. It, in Küng's words, "looks towards the kingdom of God, waits for it, or rather makes a pilgrimage towards it and is its herald, proclaiming it to the world. . . . God alone can bring his reign; the Church is devoted entirely to its service."[10]

One must admit that it is a long way from God's loving, saving, challenging intervention in history to St. Ursula or St. Praxides or any of the experiences of church we have had. We are not very good heralds nor very enthusiastic pilgrims. We are bound together by a tentative and frail, albeit positive, response to the challenge of the kingdom. But our response is not that enthusiastic commitment which can convert our communities into the love and service that makes them lights on the mountaintop—another way of saying that we are precisely the kind of men that Jesus came to preach the kingdom for: weak, fragile sinners. Indeed, we are not capable of bringing the kingdom of God; he alone can do that. Unfortunately, we have, as it turns out, been rather poor in its service.

Sometimes I think that Jesus would have been much better advised to have darkened the sun or dispersed a few Roman legions. Admittedly, if his way had produced a substantial number of followers who would imitate his loving service and unshakeable faith, it would have been great; but unfortunately he has not been able to come up with many followers who enthusiastically respond to his challenge. In the jargon of pro football, his game plan was fine but the personnel weak.

Hans Küng notes that the word *ekklesia* can be translated into modern languages to mean "congregation" or "community" or "church." Each of these words, he tells us, signifies something important about the nature of the group.

"Congregation" expresses the fact that the *ekklesia* is never merely a static institution, but one that exists through the repeated event of a concrete coming together. "Community" emphasizes that the *ekklesia* is never merely an abstract and distant super-organization of functionaries set above the concretely congregated community, but is a fellowship of people who meet regularly at a given place and a given time for a given purpose. "Church" makes it plain that the *ekklesia* is never merely a disconnected jumble of isolated and self-sufficient religious groups, but the members, united through their individual service, of an all embracing fellowship. Generally these three words, especially the last two, are interchangeable, while it remains true that "congregation" emphasizes a concrete event, "community" a constant local group, "Church" a supra-local fellowship, and hence in translating *ekklesia* different words may be chosen in different cases. But fundamentally they are interchangeable, and one may speak of a local Church as well as of a local community, and of a total comunity as well as a total Church.[11]

But is this Church, which is also a community and a congregation, that local band of believers—the St. Praxides and the St. Ursulas of history—or is it a worldwide organization? The only possible answer is that it is both. The local church is not a subdivision or a segment of the whole Church. Wherever a band of believers gather together to respond to the message of Jesus, to celebrate their unity and the Eucharist; wherever one finds the gospel, baptism, and the Lord's Supper, there is the Church of Jesus. In the local church we have the entire promise of the gospel, the total grace of the Father, the total presence of Jesus, and the total direction of the Holy Spirit. In Küng's words: "Each *ekklesia,* each congregation, community, Church, however small, however poor, however insignificant, is a full and perfect manifestation of *the ekklesia,* the congregation, the community, the Church of God."[12]

But if the whole Church is to be found in the local community, it is by no means limited to the local community. It is the Church of God in Cannes, in Ephesus, in Balihanus, in North Austin, and in Beverly Hills. The various local communities, then, are held together not merely by the fact that they have the same name, nor merely by the fact that they have some signs of external organizational union; they are held together by the fact that they are all incarnations of the same Church. In Küng's words:

All individual communities receive one and the same Gospel, all receive the same mission and the same promise. All are subject to the grace of one and the same Father, have one and the same Lord, are inspired by one and the same Holy Spirit in their charisms and their ministries. They believe one and the same faith, are sanctified by one and the same baptism, and refreshed by one and the same meal. Through all these things—and what could be more important than these?—they are not just linked together externally, but internally united; they form not just an ecclesiastical organization, but one Church.[13]

So, poor, narrow, provincial, rather drab St. Ursula manifests the same Church of God that was manifested in Jerusalem. Anxiety-ridden, sometimes racist St. Praxides is every bit as much a manifestation of the Church of God as is Rome. This is not to deny that Jerusalem or Rome have certain special and critical roles to play. (As we shall see later, it is my conviction that a papacy is indispensable.) Nevertheless, we cannot escape the fundamental truth that the kingdom of God is responded to, announced, and served at places like St. Praxides. If the Lord is to return only when the servant churches have become reasonably good at their task of heralding his Good News, we must conclude that he has a long wait ahead of him.

NOTES

1. Hans Küng, *The Church*, translated by Ray and Rosaleen Ockenden. (London: Burns & Oates, 1967), p. 44. Professor Küng's summary of the scriptural and theological thinking of the Church at the present time is probably the best available in English. Many people, both on the Left and the Right—not excluding those at the very top of the Church—are persuaded that Professor Küng is a radical. However, a very careful reading of *The Church* will reveal that Küng's position is essentially very moderate if not conservative. But "radical," "moderate," "conservative" are not appropriate titles for Hans Küng; he is a scholar and a man of faith, which is more than can be said for many of the pop theologians—and perhaps for not a few of Herr Küng's critics on the Right. In this book I lean very heavily on his thought as contained in *The Church*.

2. *Ibid.*, p. 75.

3. The word "kingdom" does not mean today what it did in the time of Jesus. Most of our kings have very little power, and most of the leaders of great nations who are not called kings have far more power than did any kings in ages past. We shall use the word

"kingdom" in this book because it is the translation still used in most versions of scripture; however, the words "power of God" will more accurately convey the notion to a modern reader. Thus, the phrase of Mark 1:15 might be revised to read, "Time is fulfilled and the Power of God is at hand. Repent and believe in the Good News."

4. The present attempts of some enthusiasts to argue that since the Church represents a religious revolution it also ought to represent a political revolution are simply foreign to all sensible interpretation of the scriptures and indeed a perversion of the Christian message. Professor Oscar Cullman in his book *Jesus and the Revolutionaries* (New York: Harper & Row, 1970) effectively disposes of these enthusiasts. It is worth noting, however, that while the Church is not a political (much less revolutionary) organization, it does not follow that Christians should stay clear of politics or that they are forbidden to even engage in revolutionary politics on occasion.

5. Joachim Jeremias, *The Parables of Jesus* (New York: Charles Scribner's Sons, 1963), p. 230.

6. Joachim Jeremias, *The Sermon on the Mount* (Philadelphia: Fortress Press [Facet Books]), 1963, p. 33.

7. *Ibid., pp.* 34–35.

8. Küng, *The Church,* p. 62.

9. *Ibid.,* p. 93.

10. *Ibid.,* pp. 95 and 96.

11. *Ibid.,* pp. 84–85.

12. *Ibid.,* p. 86.

13. *Ibid.,* p. 86.

Chapter Three

THE CHURCH AS THE PEOPLE OF GOD AND AS THE BODY OF CHRIST

People of God

The phrase "People of God" has become immensely popular in the Church since the Vatican Council. It has been used so frequently and so mindlessly that it has been turned into a slogan, a catchword, a symbol without meaning. Such a development is unfortunate because the phrase has very precise and important biblical roots. It implies that the Church is the continuation of Israel and that those who respond to God's free intervention in the person and message of Jesus are in direct continuity with those who responded to his intervention during the Exodus and at Sinai. As God's people, the Church is the object of Yahweh's free generosity. By his own gracious choice, we now belong to him, and even though we may desert our side of the covenant, he has committed himself irrevocably to us.

As the early community of the followers of Jesus began to develop its own organizational identity, the idea became more clear to them that they were the New Israel, the new people of God. It was, as Hans Küng puts it, "the oldest and most fundamental concept underlying the self-interpretation of the Church."

The Epistles of St. Paul abound in references to the

Church as the New Israel. The famous phrase of I Peter
2:9–10 summarizes most specifically the self-understanding of the Church of God's people called in mercy and now
commissioned to announce God's goodness:

> But you are *a chosen race, a royal priesthood, a consecrated nation, a people set apart* to sing the praises
> of God who called you out of the darkness into his wonderful light. Once you were *not a people* at all and now
> you are the People of God; once you were *outside the
> mercy* and now *you have been given mercy.*

One can randomly find quotes in the Epistles that repeat
this theme. (Galatians 6:16, Romans 9:6, Galatians 3:29,
Romans 9:7, Philippians 3:3, Corinthians 3:16.)

There are a number of important conclusions which follow from the notion that the Church is God's people. God
chose Israel; Israel did not choose him. We are chosen for
the Church; we do not choose it. Israel responded to God
only sporadically, but God did not turn away. Sometimes
we, as the New Israel, respond to him; at other times we
do not. Nonetheless, he does not repent of the promises he
has made. Israel was a people on pilgrimage; so, too, the
New Israel is on pilgrimage. It is not static, does not stand
still; it moves toward a goal, however slowly and lackadaisically. Israel had a history. It did not come into being
all at once, nor did it evolve in neat, orderly fashion. So,
too, the New Israel has a history. It is not merely rooted
in time and space but has moved through different times
and different spaces; and at some times in some places it
has failed miserably in responding to God's invitation.
Yves Congar summarizes beautifully the extremely important point that no nation can exist without structure and
order—Israel did not, and neither can the New Israel.

It always represents an ensemble of members, all alive

and active, all sharing the quality of dignity of the life of the body, and a structure of function with a head to assure the unity and the government of the whole. In a nation, all the citizens participate in the life of the city and exercise there their specific function. . . . In this regard, we have already seen the significance of the Chapter *de Populo Dei in genere* of the conciliar scheme *de Ecclesia*. We add here a consideration which is not by any means alien to this chapter, and which suggests the idea of the sacrament of salvation we have already mentioned. This is the People of God, structured in such a way that it carries the mission and represents in the world *the sign of salvation,* which God has constituted in a definite way, complete and sufficient by itself, *in Christo et in Ecclesia.*[1]

We have noted before that the Church can no more achieve the kingdom of God by its own efforts than the old Israel could cause the coming of the long sought Messiah. Nonetheless, the Church, the New Israel is a people of movement. It is on pilgrimage, it is active, it is marching in a direction. It has purpose and destiny. As Father Congar puts it:

The idea of the People of God introduces, therefore, something dynamic in the consideration of the Church. This People possesses a life and marches towards a goal established by God. It was chosen, instituted and consecrated by God to be His servant and His witness. The People of God is like a sacrament of salvation offered to the world. This is what we mean when we say: God, wishing (with antecedent will) the salvation of all men, has placed in the world a cause, sufficient by itself to carry out effectively this will. Thus, He has placed Jesus Christ in the world and, depending on Him and originating in Him, the Church, the messianic people, gathered according to the new and final disposition of the alliance, living by the benefits of this alliance through the means established by the Lord for that purpose. The People of

God is established by revelation, by the institutions and the sacraments of the new and the final disposition of the alliance, is in the midst of the world, and is for the world the sign and the sacrament of salvation offered by all men.[2]

There is little in the comparison with Israel that permits us to idealize the Church. Israel was holy but not by its own action; it was God's free choice. Israel was committed to God, but only because God chose it. Israel was in an unbreakable alliance with God, but only because of God's commitment. So it is with the New Israel. Its holiness comes from God not from its members. Its election is not something for which it can claim any special credit, and its permanence as God's servant people persists in spite of its own spectacular efforts to break away from his love.

The term "People of God" is frequently used with an anti-clerical tone to it. If, as the Vatican Council makes quite clear, we are all part of the *laos Theou,* which is Greek for the People of God, then it follows that everyone, priest and lay person alike, is part of God's people. We are all a holy nation, a chosen race, a royal priesthood. The laity are not distinct from the Church; they are the Church. Because we are all laity, we are all part of the *laos.* But the conclusion, which some uninformed Catholics make, that there is therefore no need of special offices or special functions in the Church is completely invalid. Indeed, there is no room for the special caste or class, for a group of men and women who are the Church in some superior sense to have control over the destinies and lives of others. No one has the right to claim that he is the Church in a special way and that others are inferior members of the Church. We are all God's people. Nevertheless, as in every people, unity and order require that there be a distinction of functions. There surely was such a distinction in Israel and there is in every people known to social science. The term "People of God" does not abolish the clergy or hierarchy, but it does remind them that they are servants rather than lords and masters. One must note, of course, that frequently in the history of the Church, indeed even in its present experience, this reminder has not been heard.

I shall return to this theme in the concluding chapter of the book, but I want to repeat once again, both for the heresy-hunters of the Right and the anti-structural enthusiasts of the Left: The Church like all human communities must have structure and organization. Indeed, one need merely read the epistles and the acts of the apostles to see that leadership, distinction of function, and established patterns of behavior emerged at the very beginning.

Body of Christ

For approximately three decades before the Vatican Council the term "Body of Christ" was as important as "People of God" has become since the Council—and it was used almost as mindlessly. Since everyone used the phrase to mean almost anything they wanted it to mean; now it means practically nothing. Indeed, it traveled the route from insight to cliche in the space of a few years. This is most unfortunate because the phrase says something extremely important about the nature of the Church as the community of those who respond to Jesus. It is not as though the Body of Christ and the People of God represent different realities; they don't. But the two phrases give us a somewhat different perspective. Hans Küng's words are especially appropriate here:

It is fundamental from every point of view to see the

Church as the people of God; this idea is found not only in Paul, but is the oldest term to describe the *ekklesia,* and it emphasizes the crucial continuity between the Church and Israel and the Old Testament. Only by seeing the Church as the people of God can we understand the idea of the Church as the body of Christ; then we shall see that the concept "body of Christ" describes very fittingly the new and unique nature of this new people of God. The Church is only the body of Christ insofar as it is the people of God; but by being the new people of God constituted by Christ it is truly the body of Christ.[3]

St. Paul uses the term Body of Christ to mean three different things. First, it is the crucified and risen body of Christ; second, it is the Lord's body present in the Lord's Supper; and finally, it is the union of the members of the Church through the Lord's Supper and the crucified and risen Jesus. By being baptized we are buried and made alive with Christ; thus, we share in the body of the crucified and risen Christ. In the Lord's Supper we identify ourselves bodily with the crucified and risen Jesus, and through that identification we become united with one another and become "one body in Christ." In other words, through baptism and, especially, through the Eucharist we are united with the crucified and risen Jesus. We are united to one another by being united with him. He is the source and the symbol of our unity, and our unity, in its turn, is a manifestation of his death and resurrection.

In St. Paul's view of things, both the local community and the worldwide Church constitute the Body of Christ. Christ is present in the individual community; he is present in the total Church. He is especially present in the Eucharist, but he is also present in the whole life of the Church. He is the source of the Church and its goal. The Church is bound together by its commitment of response to his message. The members of the Church celebrate their union with Christ through the Eucharist and by so doing deepen and ratify their union with one another. It is precisely that union in love, manifesting itself in enthusiastic service that enables the Church to be a herald of the Good News, a light shining on the mountaintop. The Church is the Body of Christ because by accepting Christ's message and by responding enthusiastically to it, it continues its work in time and space. Again, we must humbly admit that the continuation has not always been the most efficient and impressive; our faith has not been deep; our response has not been enthusiastic; our trust has not been profound; our love has not been passionate. But because we have been a pitiably inadequate Body of Christ does not mean that we are not his body. It means, rather, that there is still much work to be done.

Another Pauline image closely related to the Body of Christ image serves as a fitting summary to our reflections on what the New Testament has to say about the Church. St. Paul, searching for an analogy to convey both the intensity and the intimacy of the relationship between Jesus and the new People of God, turned to the union between husband and wife. The sexual union, the most passionate, most demanding, most overpowering of human relationships, symbolized in St. Paul's mind both the way Jesus felt about his Church and the way the Church ought to respond to Jesus' love.

We have insisted repeatedly in this volume that the Church is a web of human relationships, a group of men and women trying desperately to break out of the lonely isolation of their own alienation and break through with love and trust in one another. We have said that such a thrust toward unity is to be found in all human religious communities and that what makes Christianity different is not its quest for unity but rather the basis upon which it believes unity is possible. Note that the four New Testament symbols we have used are all relational—kingdom, people, body, marriage—all represent deep, powerful, primordial unions. The message of Jesus, in other words, is that God has intervened to overcome the suspicion, distrust, conflict, and hatred which have separated individuals from one another.

The Christian believes that unity is possible in his community and, through his community, in the whole human race, because God has intervened to promise and guarantee that unity. He also believes that he bears witness to this intervention of God precisely to the extent that his relationship with others is an imitation of God's love for him. "As I have loved you, so you love one another . . . by this shall all men know that you are my disciples, that you have love for one another." The Christian is committed to the notion that the profound, tender, passionate, patient, sensitive, comforting love between a man and a woman who are deeply in love with one another ought to be the model for all human relationships. He realizes how difficult this is even in marriage and how much more difficult it is in other human relationships. But he knows that the only way his faith community can become the light on the mountaintop is by its members' living lives of profound love, a love which would be not only absurd but impossible if God had not intervened through Jesus. Those who are not part of the Church will believe in God's intervention only when the passion radiating from the Body of Christ is so powerful that no other explanation can be imagined.

NOTES

1. Yves Congar, O. P., *This Church That I Love* (New York: Dimension Books, 1969), p. 24.

2. *Ibid.*, p. 19.

3. Kung, *The Church*, p. 225.

Chapter Four

THE CHURCH AND THE VATICAN
COUNCIL

This book is not the place for a long and detailed history of how the Constitution on the Church at the second Vatican Council developed. It is sufficient to say that it is a revolutionary document insofar as it focused attention not so much on the Church's juridic structure as on its nature as a people and a community. This change of focus may have been the most important theoretical contribution of the Council, although its full implications have yet to be felt in the life of the Church.

We discussed in the previous chapter the concept of the People of God which the Constitution on the Church restored to its proper place in Christian thought. In this chapter, some things must be said about another notion treated by the Council fathers—the Church as the "universal sacrament of salvation."

In the very first paragraph of the Conciliar document, *Lumen Gentium,* the Council fathers note: "By her relationship with Christ, the Church is a kind of sacrament or sign of intimate union with God and of the unity of all mankind." At first reading such a sentence may seem to smack of the pompous triumphalism which the Vatican Council was supposed to have terminated. However, if the sentence is read in the context of all the things which have already been said in this book, one can understand that the title "universal sacrament of salvation" is more of a challenge to the Church than a prerogative about which it can afford to be complacent.

First of all, the Church is the sign of salvation for the whole world not on its own merits but because of its union with Christ. *He* is the one who came to preach the Father's decisive intervention in human affairs. *He* is the one who bore witness to God's love for men. *He* is the one who demands that we serve one another even as he served us. It is *his* death and resurrection into which we are baptized. It is union with *him* that we celebrate in the Eucharist. The Church is the sign of *him* insofar as it responds to the challenge *he* has come to offer. And, as the community of those who respond, the Church necessarily represents, however imperfectly, the challenge that Jesus offers the world.

Nor is the salvation of which the Church is a sign something totally other-worldly. It is the whole of God's creation, material as well as physical, which was redeemed by God's intervention through Jesus. Father Congar summarizes the present understanding of theologians about the meaning of salvation:

> *What is salvation?* Without discarding what it might have of truth, we must obviously go beyond the idea of a mere rescue of individual souls in the way some survivors are saved from a shipwreck, where the rest of the passengers are lost. This simile does not take into account the situation and the role of man in the world, nor of the unity of God's plan and work, nor the testimonies of the Holy Scripture on the cosmic character of Redemption. If it is true that the present consideration of the state of man has developed and has a prominent place, we can speak of the link between man and the cosmos, and of the unity of the universe. The world is made of only one material, and man physically participates in that material, al-

though he surpasses the world because of his personal conscience. In man the universe reaches a hypostatic or personal dignity. Thus man, being connected with the world, transforms it. The union among them is such that, in man and through men, the cosmos accomplishes its purpose. This is a union of destiny, based at the same time on God's unity of plan in his communications *ad extra*, and on the real unity of the universe, the perception of which is no doubt the inspiring principle of Fr. Teilhard de Chardin's views. Salvation is not merely the rescue of some survivors, but the consummation in God of all his visible creation, together with man who is the crowning and the immanent goal.[1]

Father Congar's position is not surprising until we stop to consider that I am claiming that St. Praxides and St. Ursula are the Church. One is prepared to concede that the Church is a sign of salvation, a sign that God's love is consummated in all his physical creation together with man "who is the crowning and the immanent goal." But St. Praxides or St. Ursula as symbols of the unity of the universe in God? Obviously, the eyes of faith have to be terribly perceptive to see it. But the point is not that the local church is a particularly good sign of salvation; it is, rather, that it is the best sign we have, indeed, the only one. If the local church realizes what it is supposed to be and compares that ideal with what it is, the result ought to be not so much triumphalist complacency but a profound humility and, as we used to say in the old catechisms, a firm purpose of amendment.

A man with the eyes of faith believes that God has intervened in human history through Jesus and is committed by his belief to the notion that God intends that the disunity which separates mankind be replaced by unity. He is also committed to the conviction that the Church is a sign of such unity, however poor and inadequate. If the local parish is the Church manifested in a particular segment of time and place, it ought to manifest the sort of unity which God wills with the whole human race. As Jan Groot put it:

> This unity and peace is, therefore, not based on one or the other particular form of human society but on that fellowship which is embodied in Christ as the new man and which, through him, is sacramentally present in the Church. It is a unity and peace "in Christ." Thus communion with Christ and through him with the Father is the root of that human unity which really tends towards peace. Therefore any genuine and saving unity and peace in human history must be related by their nature to Christ and his Church. They must tend from within towards that explicit embodiment which is already vicariously present in the Church as the Body of Christ on behalf of the whole world.[2]

The point is not so much that the relationships within a local community of Christians are going to "cause" the unity of the whole human race; the quality of the relationships ought to be a sign to the world outside that unity is possible among men, and possible precisely insofar as men accept God's intervention in human history as manifested in Jesus.

There are, then, two ways that the Christian works for human unity: He strives to overcome all the barriers of suspicion and distrust that stand in the way of men's love for each other; and by the quality of his own relationships, particularly in the local community of Christians, he stands as a sign to other men that friendship and trust are possible. Let us emphasize once again that the Christian's life as a sign of the possible unity of mankind does not make him a better person. It it not a special prerogative; it is rather a responsibility and a challenge that his faith imposes upon him.

Father Schillebeeckx observes: "Human unity in its essence is not a mere datum; it is a test to be carried out." He goes on to say:

> Mankind, then, has received salvation through the fraternal service on one chosen from among ourselves—Jesus Christ, the Elect of God, the Son of the Father. This fact of Christ, which took place in our history and in our secular and human affairs, has had a real effect on human history. Mankind's new fundamental but real unity and new structure as a community rests upon God's universal saving will. This will is not an actuality that is simply beyond history; it has manifested itself visibly within history in the "objective redemption," that is, in the personal life of Jesus, representative man, Son of God, appearing among us in our history.[3]

Father Schillebeeckx's remarks underline the most difficult paradox of Christianity. We come together in a local church to find unity with those with whom we are convinced we share common values, and the most fundamental of those values is that we must work for the unity of the whole human race; therefore we are obliged to transcend the limitations and the boundaries of the local parish. If we do not engage in the struggle for unity beyond the boundaries of the local community, then unity within the local group is seriously threatened, precisely because we are not honoring that fundamental principle which has brought us together. In the final analysis, St. Ursula and St. Praxides—and any Christian community—will stand or fall on their ability to move beyond themselves.

It is a nice question as to how many members of the local community must be actively engaged in the task of removing barriers to human unity to ensure that the parish itself will not die of the stagnation that comes from infidelity. What proportion of the local community must be engaged in the "secular" search for unity so that the parish might be true to itself? God is neither a mathematician nor a social scientist, and thus far in human history he has indicated a willingness to settle for a saving remnant. Nonetheless, if there is practically no one in a local church of Christians concerned about the world beyond, then that local church is a poor sign of God's intervention in history through Christ. It is a poor response to the Good News Christ came to bring.

The Christian may be one with his non-Christian colleagues in his deep involvement in the task of bringing unity to mankind, yet he is operating with another and a deeper motive. In Schillebeeckx's words:

> Christianity means not only communion with God in the concrete milieu of Christ in his Church, but also *working* with the living God, with the Father "who is ever active" (John 5:17) both in the Church and in the world. Religion is primarily personal intercourse with God—the living God, who is the Creator of men and things, all of which he offers to us for humanization. Therefore, our living relationship with our neighbor and with the world is not only cultural but also religious.

> *Agape* embraces God and men. Love of God cannot and must not be separated from love of men. Christian love for the neighbor means that we—God and I—love *my* fellow-men. While in natural human love, God is present only in silence as the transcendent Third, my Christian *caritas* towards my fellows is just as much love, but a love lived in communion with God. And so the Christian loves his fellow man with the same love as that with which he loves God and with which both he and his fellowmen are loved by God. In Christ alone do we learn the proper meaning of "being a man for the sake of others," although secular and human experience will teach us how we must express this fellowship in concrete situations.[4]

This observation is extremely important. Those who engage in social reform movements can in their zeal and enthusiasm and commitment become harsh, self-righteous, and fanatic. It is easy to persuade ourselves that the quality of human life and human relationship can be improved only if we *impose* such an improvement. We will force men to be free. But if there is one lesson in human history, it is that, as T. S. Eliot puts it, "When good does evil in order to accomplish good, it becomes indistinguishable from the evil it is fighting." When in the name of love we engage in hatred, then we destroy the love which we claim to be promoting. The Christian realizes, or at least ought to realize, that this course is not open to him. He also realizes, or ought to realize, that unity among men is something God grants. He is thereby not excused from working, but he is excused from assuming a kind of total responsibility for unity, which is usually the prelude to dogmatic self-righteousness. The Christian does not permit himself to become a zealot because he knows that zealotry is false to the style of life demanded of him and because he knows that in the long run zealotry is self-defeating. In attempting to impose the unity that only God can produce, the zealot, in effect, makes himself the equivalent of God.

The local parish, then, is a base of operations. It is the community in a given time and place of those who believe in the message of Jesus, who respond to the challenge of God's intervention in history, and who commit themselves to lives in which they will be a sign of God's love not only within the brotherhood of the faithful but in the entire world. As Father Schillebeeckx notes: "The Church therefore will appear as a sign among men actually drawing and inviting them only when the love of her members for humankind becomes concretely and historically visible here and now."[5] We cannot claim that God and Christ are limited to working through the Church. Obviously, they are free to work wherever they wish, and just as obviously there are many who are not formal members of a community of Christians who in fact do respond to the message of God's loving intervention in history, although not necessarily explicitly and consciously. For the Church to claim an exclusive role as a sign and an instrument of God would be grossly triumphalist. One does not presume to budget the Holy Spirit's time for him. The local churches are not the only signs of human unity and surely not the best possible signs. All that can be claimed for them is that the local churches and the Church as it manifests itself there are the official and explicit signs of that salvation which is unity. The extent to which they fail to be adequate signs is not the measure of the weakness of the message but rather the measure of the weakness of the response to the message. Or as G. K. Chesterton put it, "It's not that Christianity has been tried and found wanting, but found hard and not tried."

In the process of developing and articulating the ideas contained in this book, I encountered objections from two sets of people. The first set argues that the Church has no right to claim a monopoly on salvation; the second, that however splendid and beautiful are my theories of the Church as People of God, Body of Christ, Messianic Herald, and Sign of Salvation, the factual reality of the Church is filled with so much stupidity, incompetence, narrowness, and corruption that it cannot be taken seriously as fulfilling any of these symbols.

It has always seemed to me that I had taken these arguments into account. I made no claim that the Church is the only source of salvation, nor do I attempt to argue that the local parish is without flaw or blemish. But the objections persist; I suspect because of attitudes and perspectives that were formed for many of us in our early catechetical experiences. No one told us in so many words that the Catholic Church was perfect, but its style of responding to objections and justifying actions could easily lead us to think that it was. Surely the Church wasn't eager to admit its mistakes. Those mistakes it did admit were more or less presumed to have stopped with the death of Cesare Borgia or at some other point in the remote past. Neither did we say that there was absolutely no salvation outside the Church, and yet it was very easy to get the impression that the operation of God and his Spirit beyond the boundaries of the Church was a rather exceptional phenomenon. Neither of these attitudes is particularly acceptable to men of our time. The conviction is widespread even among Catholics that somehow or other the Catholic Church is committed to both positions. (And it is useful for many Catholics to think so. They can expend considerable energy tilting at those windmills, thereby justifying the absence of any other religious behavior in their lives.)

I have insisted in this volume that the Church's role is to be the sign and the symbol of God's unifying salvation. To fulfill that role is an obligation and a responsibility, not a privilege or a prerogative. The inadequacy of the Church as a sign is built into it as a community made up of human beings, which is, if not cheerfully at least humbly, acknowledged by the Church. The Church may not be a very good sign; it may not be a very adequate community of those who respond to the message of Jesus and the intervention of God; however, it is in fact the only communal response that exists. The local church is the only assembly of people who have accepted and committed themselves publicly and explicitly to the intervention of God in history represented by Jesus. It can claim no more and it can strive for no less.[6]

But there is also something absurd about the armchair

critic who gleefully points out all the weaknesses of the Church as though it were something distinct from himself. If the Church has failed to be a very effective sign, the reason is that Christians have not been very effective as Christians. The expert may soothe his conscience by scapegoating the hierarchy for his own failures; but the hierarchy is not the Church—though a part of it. The pastor of the local parish is not the Church—though a part of it. The Church is the community of Christians, and the local church is the manifestation of the community in a given section of time and space.

The most effective means of improving the Church—and its impact is guaranteed—is for the individual critic to become a better Christian, a deeper man of faith, a more open man of love, a more generous man in the service of unity inside the Church and in the whole world. The failures of the Church are not just the failures of the hierarchy—though these are important failures. The Church has failed to be all that it ought to be because Christians have failed to be all that they ought to be. Those young enthusiasts who say so confidently that the Church is irrelevant fail to realize that the question is not whether the Church is relevant but whether they are. If they are relevant, then the Church will be because they are the Church. If they push the matter further and say that the fundamental questions are whether the message of Jesus is at all pertinent in our time and whether the intervention of God in history is credible in our time, we are forced to agree with them. The message is indeed impertinent and intervention is incredible. But there is no reason to believe that it is more impertinent and more incredible today than it has ever been. It was once a stumbling block to the Jews and a folly to the Gentiles. Is it any different for us? Man must decide either to accept it or reject it. If they accept it, they must band together with others who accept it to live lives which bear witness to it; and this band is called the Church.

If one is already part of such a band and discovers that many of those in positions of leadership are less than adequate for the responsibilities of their positions, it makes no sense to leave. There is no place else to go.

Or, as one colleague of mine put it, "Why leave? Stay and bother them."

NOTES

1. Congar, pp. 44–45.
2. Jan Groot, "The Church as Sacrament of the World." *Concilium*, Vol. 1, No. 4, January, 1968, p. 30.
3. Edward Schillebeeckx, O.P., "The Church and Mankind." *Concilium*, Vol. 1, No. 1, January, 1965, p. 36.
4. *Ibid.*, p. 48.
5. *Ibid.*, p. 47.
6. I do not propose to discuss in the present volume the complicated question of unity within the Church and will therefore not devote any attention to the question of whether the Church of God is manifested not merely in St. Praxides but also in Faith Lutheran Church two blocks away.

Chapter Five

LEADERSHIP AND THE CHURCH STRUCTURE

W e carried away from our religion classes the notion that Jesus left some sort of blueprint for his followers which contained in schematic form the shape of the Church at the time of the First Vatican Council. All history did was to fill in a few details. Actually, however, most of the structures of the Church as we know them emerged through an evolutionary process. Such evolutions are not false to Jesus' original instruction, but they are not part of the divine institution of the Church to the extent that Jesus clearly and explicitly spelled them out.

Raymond E. Brown, the distinguished Catholic scripture scholar, points out that there were four different roles in the primitive Church out of which the present structure of the priesthood emerged.[1] There was first of all the "disciple," a man who was bound in a special way to the ministry of Jesus. He is simply a committed follower of Jesus, whether he has any functional roles in the institution or not.

Secondly, there is the "apostle," who is essentially a servant. Father Brown points out that we must not introduce into the New Testament era notions of service that have developed in modern times. While Paul certainly thinks of himself as a servant, his primary emphasis in apostleship is not service to others but service to Jesus

Christ. The Pauline concept of apostleship includes the service of ordinary work, by which Paul earned his own living lest he be a burden to his converts, the service of collecting money, the service of prayer, the service of suffering, the service of correction, and, of course, the service of preaching the gospel.

Thirdly, there was the "presbyter-bishop," the man who was responsible for the pastoral care of the churches. He was, in a sense, an agent left in charge by the apostle when he went on to continue his service of Jesus Christ in other cities. He was not simply the dedicated Christian as the disciple was, nor was he a wandering missionary like an apostle; he was, rather, the pastor of a local church. This does not mean that he was either a priest or a bishop in the contemporary meaning of those terms.

Finally, there was the one who presided over the Eucharist. As Father Brown remarks: "It is significant that the New Testament does not attribute much Eucharistic functioning to any of the three roles we have already discussed." Apparently, some bishops presided over the Eucharist and some of those who presided over it were not bishops. According to Father Brown: "We are never told anywhere in the New Testament that any of the twelve followers of Jesus ever presided over the Lord's Supper."

These points are not made to suggest that in the present day someone other than a priest or bishop could preside over the Eucharist; rather, we mention these points in order to stress that the structures of the Church we have today, as well as those which finally emerged toward the end of the first century, developed gradually and organically out of the message of Jesus. They were not laid down in a clear and precise blueprint. The combination of the four roles we have described into a model of the priesthood is perfectly valid and has been an immense help throughout the development of the Church; whether new models could also begin to develop is not a question especially appropriate to this book. However, on the basis of Father's Brown research, one is forced to say that there is no reason, at least in sacred scripture, to prevent new models from emerging. On the other hand, it also ought to be clear that there is no reason in the scripture to say that new models should develop. There is much less reason to say that individuals on their own initiative do anything but harm to themselves and the Church if they begin to "play around" with creating new structures to meet what they think are their needs. Nevertheless, it must still be emphasized that the New Testament experience does show that there is not just one way in which the people of God, who are also the Body of Christ, must be organized.

Dean Colin Williams in his book, *The Church*, quotes the passage in Acts 2:42: "They devoted themselves to the apostles' teaching and fellowship, to the breaking of bread and the prayers." In trying to get at what is of the absolute essence in the structure of the Church, he comments: "Included in this statement are three institutional characteristics: (a) The church depends for its being upon *the apostolic message;* (b) the church continues as *an apostolic fellowship;* (c) the church centers its life around *a particular form of cultus.*[2]

First, then, as we have said before, the Church exists essentially as a response to the message of Jesus. If it is not a response to and a continuation of that message, then it is no longer the Church. While the message may shape different structures of the Church in different times and places, the message is still the essence of the Church, and the whole community exists essentially to propogate it.

But it is also a community of fellows—in King Hal's words in *Henry V,* "a band of brothers." The message is not being handed on by isolated individuals but rather by a community of friends who are opening their friendship to all the world. In Dean Williams' words:

> A further and more important aspect of apostolic fellowship seems evident. We have seen how the Pentecost story centers on the creation of a fellowship in which the barriers of race, language, and culture fell beneath the powerful awareness of a new unity in Christ given them by the Spirit. This fellowship was the climactic act of the redemptive drama to which the apostles were witness. The fellowship in which they shared was a gift offered to the broken communities of the earth.[3]

Finally, the earliest manifestation of the Church was at a worship communion. The breaking of bread together was a sign and symbol of the unity which existed among the members. It was also a rededication to continue the preaching of the message. It represented the belief of the early Christians that someday they would eat the banquet of the Eucharist once again with the Lord.

The preaching of the gospel, the fellowship of Christians, the Eucharistic assembly—these are the very minimal structures of the Church. Where preaching the gospel is deemed irrelevant, or the Eucharist a waste of time, or community with others of like conviction thought to be only of marginal help, then one no longer has the Christian Church.

To list these three "marks" of the Church is not at all to imply that other elements of Church structure are not essential or, indeed, are not of divine origin (although one must specify, mostly to the theologians and to the historians and scripture scholars, precisely in what sense they are of divine origin). Rather, we describe these three marks to emphasize that it is for the preaching of the gospel, development of community, and the celebration of the Eucharist that necessarily all the other structures exist. The People of God who are the Body of Christ are not a means to the end of ecclesiastical structure. Quite the contrary, ecclesiastical structure serves as a means to the end of the building up of the People of God and the expansion of the Body of Christ. Any other approach to Church structure completely misses the point of the reason why the Church came to be.

One of the great difficulties we have in understanding the meaning of the Church, or indeed the meaning of any aspect of Christianity, is the impression that most of us obtained during our formative years that everything was settled. There were no unsolved theological questions in the Church; indeed, there was not even any reason to try to reformulate language. All the insights had occurred long ago; all the symbols had been developed; everything that needed to be said was said.

Then the Second Vatican Council happened and suddenly we discovered there were many things we did not fully understand; many insights were indeed possible, many symbols could be explored much more deeply, and our grasp of Christianity could be richer and fuller. But while this discovery was exciting, it was also puzzling, both because we didn't quite know what to do with the insights of the past and we weren't sure how to cope with the symbols we thought we understood as we plunged deeper into their meaning. We can see, for example, that the idea of leadership runs through the whole New Testament. Certain men were to assume special responsibilities among Jesus' followers both during his own ministry and after his departure to the Father. We have also come to understand that leadership can take many different forms in the Church. Finally, we realize that there is absolutely no theological necessity for the style of the exercise of the

offices of the papacy and hierarchy to be for all times what
they were in 1940.

Now we understand that the whole question of theology
in the history of leadership in the Church is in great need
of profound examination. The Constitution on the Church
or the Vatican Council statement on collegiality will be
seen, I suspect, from the point of view of future historians,
not as the end of a long discussion about the nature of
leadership in the Church but only as the beginning.

Nevertheless, while the discussion goes on, the Church
must have leaders and we need some serviceable concepts
for dealing with the phenomenon of leadership in the
Church. I propose to look at leadership in general and in
the Church from the viewpoint of a sociologist. Without
trying to resolve any of the complicated historical or theological questions about the papacy or the hierarchy, I will
address myself to the question of what the most appropriate styles might be at the present time for the exercise of
leadership in the Church.

Leadership for the Present

When the sociologist learns from the exegete and the
theologian that the Church must have leadership, he is not
surprised, because there is no human organization that can
survive for long without it. That there are some special
qualities for ecclesiastical leadership which cannot be
found in other human organizations is a question beyond
the scope of the sociologist. He is, however, in a position
to say that insofar as the Church is a large corporate organization working in the modern world, it necessarily has
leadership problems similar to those of other large corporate organizations. Indeed, it can be said more strongly:
whatever theoretical explanation or justification there may

be for leadership, those who occupy leadership positions in large organizations have the same kinds of problems and the same kinds of challenges, and must respond with the same sorts of leadership styles.

So the concept of leadership which I am going to describe in this section is one that need not be limited to the Church. I would argue that it is one of the missions of the Church to lead the way in developing patterns of leadership which are appropriate both to the problems of our highly complex society and to the deep yearnings of the human personality for meaningful relationships in the midst of large corporate structures. The Church's leadership style should be a light shining on the mountaintop to show others that leadership can be effective and at the same time humane.

Professor John Schaar describes the kind of humane leadership (as opposed to bureaucratic) that is demanded both by the militant personalism of the New Left and by the requisites of effectively functioning organizations:

> Humanly significant leadership bases its claim to authority on a kind of knowledge which includes intuition, insight, and vision as indispensable elements. The leader strives to grasp and to communicate the essence of a situation in one organic and comprehensive conception. He conjoins elements which the analytic mind keeps tidily separate. He unites the normative with the empirical, and promiscuously mixes both with the moral and the esthetic. The radical distinction between subjective and objective is unknown in this kind of knowledge, for everything is personal and comes from within the prepared consciousness of the knower, who is simultaneously believer and actor. When it is about men, this kind of knowledge is again personal. It strives to see within the self and along with other selves. It is knowledge of character and destiny. . . .

The language in which the knowledge appropriate to humanly significant leadership is expressed is also very different from the language of rational and objective discourse. It is a language profuse in illustration and anecdote, and rich in metaphor whose sources are the human body and the dramas of action and responsibility. This language is suggestive and alluring, pregnant, evocative —in all ways the opposite of the linear, constricted, jargonized discourse which is the ideal of objective communication. Decisions and recommendations are often expressed in parables and visions whose meanings are hidden to outsiders but translucent to those who have eyes to see. Teaching in this language is done mainly by story, example, and metaphor-modes of discourse which can probe depths of personal being inaccessible to objective and managerial discourse. Compare the Sermon on the Mount with the latest communique from the Office of Economic Opportunity in the War on Poverty, or Lincoln's Second Inaugural with Nixon's first.[4]

Let it be noted carefully what Schaar is saying. He insists not merely that this is a humanly desirable kind of leadership but that it is functionally necessary if large corporate structures (government, labor, education, and church) are not going to become monstrous machines running out of control. Schaar thinks there is a choice between Abbie Hoffman and Robert McNamara; but the third alternative is not one for which many models exist. I do not think it is too unrealistic to demand that a Church whose founder claimed that leadership was friendship be in the vanguard in the development of such a model.

I shall now turn to a more detailed description of what the functions of leadership in the Church (indeed, any human organization) are.

I. *Symbolic Leadership*

The human need for leaders who incarnate the goals,

values, and elan of an organization is powerful and probably permanent. An effective leader must be "transparent." That is to say, his commitment to the values and goals of the organization must be such that the members can see in him the personification of what the organization is striving for. What is required, one suspects, is not a special kind of personal attractiveness but rather a clear, enthusiastic and articulate commitment to goals. The great men of the sixties such as John Kennedy and Martin Luther King were not Pied Pipers; they were men whose convictions and commitments were unmistakable. Man seems to need in his leaders evidence that they "really believe" the things they say, and that they really have confidence that the goals they describe can be achieved. The mass media do not seem to be able to "merchandise" this quality.

There is no room in the symbolic leader for self-pity or handwringing, for indecisiveness or hedging of bets. He must have courage, wit, hope, and the willingness to take risks. He must be able to channel energies and enthusiasms instead of trying to restrain them.

The symbolic leader plays both a prophetic and therapeutic role, which is to say, he both challenges and comforts. He bestirs his followers from their lethargy, complacency, and self-satisfaction. He is not satisfied with the way things are, and he demands of those associated with him that they use the best of their talents. On the other hand, he is not a prophet in the sense of Amos' denunciations or Jeremiah's sitting on the edge of the city calling down imprecations. He is able to comfort, to reassure, to strengthen, to support. If he says to his followers that certain things must be done, he also says they are capable of doing them. His prophecy is never such as to make his associates feel inadequate; on the contrary, it is designed to make them feel more adequate than ever before.

II. *Ideological Leadership*

The leader sees the "big picture;" he must be aware of both the overall needs of his organization and of the values and traditions which constitute its ideology. His associates are involved in their own specific tasks and needs; they are not normally inclined to look beyond them. It is the leader's role, then, to prevent their turning in on themselves and their own immediate problems and preoccupations. He is *not* a man who provides answers—a relatively easy but quite futile task. He is a man who assumes the responsibility to ask the right questions, to point out the relationships between the group's values and the "big picture," which will force the other members to think through their beliefs and their obligations. He poses problems not solutions.

In addition, the leader rejects incomplete answers; those which do not take into account either the ideology of the organization or the reality of the problems it faces. Thus, the Kennedys rejected an answer to the Cuban missile crisis which would have involved a surprise attack on Cuba because it was false to the American tradition. Similarly, one would suppose that a religious leader would reject any response to contemporary problems of sexuality which would ignore the need to respect human life. I suggest that the religious leader would ask, "What does our insight into the meaning of sexuality imply for our religious beliefs and behavior?" Then he should permit his colleagues to attempt an answer on their own rather than impose a solution on his own initiative. It takes no great skill to provide answers, but to ask the right questions, to distinguish between answers that are adequate and those that are not requires a great deal of skill. Unfortunately, we do not yet seem to have much of this skill in the Roman Church.

III. *Interpersonal*

The leader realizes that in the complex world in which we live he can ill afford to lose any of the talents of the members of his group. He therefore must create an atmosphere in which there is the greatest possibility for his individual colleagues to develop their talents to the maximum. This means not only guaranteeing them the greatest degree of freedom possible within the group but also creating an atmosphere of harmony and social support among his colleagues. Basic to this, or course, is his obligation to protect the rights of members of the group; also, he must do all that he can to see that the conflicts and the strains which exist among them are honestly and openly worked out. Conflict and tension cannot be eliminated from the human condition, but their negative effects can be minimized both by bringing conflicts into the open and by providing for everyone a sufficient amount of personal security, so that every new conflict does not seem to be an attack on the core of anyone's personality.

The interpersonal skills that are required of the leader might be compared to the socio-emotional role traditionally attributed to the mother of the family, for it has been assumed that the mother is the one who is responsible for harmonizing difficulties, healing hurts, protecting rights, and facilitating the development of talent. I would note, however, that in the best of modern families, the father shares in the socio-emotional leadership just as the mother shares in the task-oriented leadership.

IV. *Organizational*

Despite the naive romanticism of our young (and some of our not so young), no group of human beings could function for very long without organizational effort. The leader, then, must either be an administrator or see that administration gets done. Administration may be less important for leadership than symbolizing the goals and values in an organization or interpreting its ideology or creating an effective interpersonal environment. This does not mean that it is unimportant. Because some ecclesiastical leaders have, alas, equated administration with leadership does not mean that we can now have ecclesiastical groups in which administration is taboo.

The leader must, first of all, obtain the consent of his colleagues for the major decisions that the group makes. Effective authority is, in the final analysis, the ability to obtain consent. Just as it is easy to give answers, so it is easy to give orders. But orders and answers can be ignored, particularly when one does not have a secular arm available to enforce them. However divine one may be persuaded one's power is, it still is useless unless it is accepted by those toward whom it is being directed. A leader who is not able to obtain the consent of a very large majority of his colleagues on a given policy matter has failed as a leader, no matter how noble the title he may claim. Not only does the leader pose the right questions, he also presides over the dialogue which will foster responses to the questions. He realizes that everyone ought to have some kind of participation in the making of decisions. If any substantial part of the membership is excluded from the decision-making, the chances of successful implementation are minimal.

Secondly, the leader must direct and coordinate the activities of his colleagues so that the maximum result is obtained with the minimum of effort in the implementation of any decision. It is not, for example, necessary to convene a meeting of the whole group to determine whether stamps should be purchased. (In one convent I know, a twenty-minute discussion was held each day before Mass to decide which hymns were to be sung.) In other words, the leader must see to the "bookkeeping" and "housekeeping" details. It is an onerous and perhaps thankless task, and his colleagues may grumble and complain about the need to be concerned over such details. Certainly they would grumble and complain much louder if the leader failed to provide an organizational climate which provided some stability and order.

Finally, the leader must see that the organization is arranged in such a way as to maximize "pluraformity" among the various subgroups within it. For just as the talents of the individuals are developed when they have the greatest possible amount of freedom, so the contribution of subgroups will be most effective when they, too, enjoy the greatest possible amount of initiative, responsibility and structural flexibility. Just as it would be disastrous for an organization if everybody behaved exactly the same, so it would be disastrous if each subgroup within an organization was under obligation to follow one and only one model. Pluraformity is messy, inconvenient, and fits poorly on an organizational chart, but in its absence, vitality, variety, ingenuity, and creativity vanish. Perhaps the worst thing about Max Weber's bureaucrats is that they are so uniform. Given the strain towards routinization and uniformity in the modern world, the leader preserves pluraformity only if he is willing to take positive action to promote, facilitate, and guarantee variety and flexibility. He cannot assume, at least not in the present state of evolution of the species, that pluraformity will be constructive, but he can be sure that the alternative to it is apathy.

Without trying to prejudge the complex theological questions which are presently being debated about the nature of leadership in the Church, I still think it's safe to assert that, from the sociological viewpoint, the leader, whether he be the head of the whole Church or of the local Church as it is manifested in a city or a small neighborhood community (or even a tiny informal community), must view himself as the man who symbolizes the Christian message, who asks pertinent and challenging questions in the light of that message, who encourages and reassures the members of the community, and who, finally, sees that the bookkeeping and housekeeping matters are satisfied. Note well that while I put the bookkeeping and housekeeping functions at the end of my list, I do not exclude them; I think they are required in all human communities, and it is pretty hard, after having read the New Testament, to want to exclude them from the Church.

But if administration is essential, it is also not an end in itself. It exists, rather, to facilitate the work of the whole community and the exercise of the other three dimensions of the leadership role. If administration becomes an end in itself, as it so easily can and so frequently has, then a subtle and ultimately destructive perversion may slip into the Church, a perversion which is all the more dangerous in a country like the United States where the business executive represents a model of masculine leadership against which all other men are judged.[5]

I wish to emphasize once again that my plea is not for the elimination of leadership in the Church and not for the elimination of Church structures but for their improvement. Many naive Catholics assume that democracy will come to the Church when all leadership has been eliminated, despite the fact that the long history of the success of American democracy shows that it functions most effectively when leadership is strong and dynamic. One can put the matter even more forcefully. A leader in the present society who does not have some kind of democratic legitimacy cannot be a strong leader. Similarly, if democracy does not have strong leadership, it cannot survive very long as a democracy. An interesting example is leadership in the Methodist Church. The Methodist bishop is elected for a limited term. Yet while he is bishop his powers, which are clearly defined, are in many respects much stronger than those of a Catholic bishop. Many Catholic bishops today are not able to effectively lead their followers because they do not have any base of democratic consensus for their authority. The whole lesson of American democracy is that effective authority depends upon the consent of the governed. On the other hand, if there is no effective authority in a society, the result is anarchy and chaos and their inevitable consequence, authoritarianism.

The style of authority I have described in this chapter is more effective than the present mode of exercising authority in the Church. I would also like to modestly suggest to the theologians that it does seem to be somewhat more in keeping with the style of authority exercised in the New Testament.

Finally, a word must be said about the relationship between laity and clergy in the Church. All Christians are part of the *laos,* that is to say, of the People of God. The clergy are simply those who have the special functions necessary for building up the People of God. They are, as was insisted repeatedly in the New Testament, the servants of the community not the overlords. The Church cannot dispense with them; their role is essential. But, on the other hand, they are not a separate caste leading lives isolated from the rest of the people. They are not a sacred clique like the priesthood in some other religions. They are not a power elite having the right to make all important decisions by themselves—no matter how often they may have acted both like a sacred caste and a power elite.

It is probably inevitable that there will be tensions, if not conflicts, between the clergy and the nonclergy in the Church. It is also probably inevitable that the clergy will tend to develop certain common interests which they do not share with the laity. But the establishment of a separate clerical culture in which priests live and work and shape their values (with a warning, as we were given in the seminary, of the risks of friendship with lay people) must surely be considered a misunderstanding of the message of Christ if not a shameful abuse. Furthermore, a conceptualization of the Church in terms of a constant class conflict and struggle between clergy and laity may well be an interesting exercise in Marxist dialectic but it is completely foreign to the Christian message. The present situation in which many clergy and laity are almost obsessed by the clergy/laity distinction, in which some laity see no role for themselves in the Church, is one that comes into being by defining what clergy cannot do. As a historical development, it can only be regretted.

The People of God have every right to demand that their priests be dedicated, enthusiastic, holy men wherever the priest is a religious leader. If the lay people are dissatisfied when their religious leader refuses to act religiously or as a leader, they have every right to be dissatisfied. The present identity crisis of the clergy all too frequently becomes an excuse for immature confused men to escape facing the responsibilities of the commitments they have made. Some articulate Catholic spokesmen have, in effect, called for the abolition of the priesthood. This responds nicely to the "cop-out" of the clerical identity crisis. But far more Catholics are calling, inarticulately perhaps, for a priesthood that really leads, for a priesthood that is willing to run the risk of friendship with the community. Some priests see their mission in life as being irrelevant, but they do so in the face of overwhelming evidence that the vast majority of lay people, while dissatisfied with the artificial distinctions engendered by a clerical culture, still want religious leadership as much if not more than they did in the past.

In years to come the present crisis of leadership in the Church, which exists both in theory and in practice, will probably be seen as a turning point—a time of great insight and development—when notions of leadership which were developed in different cultures to meet different needs, were updated to respond to the problems of a new era, while at the same time the meaning of leadership in the Church was better understood than ever before. However, for those of us who must live through this crisis of transition, the situation is frequently awkward and painful. All the more reason then for us to keep before our eyes the image of leadership represented by a man who said he came not to be served but to serve, and then said, "I do not call you servants. I call you friends."

NOTES

1. Raymond E. Brown, *Priest and Bishop: Biblical Reflections* (New York: Paulist Press, 1970).

2. Colin W. Williams, *New Directions in Theology Today: The Church* (Philadelphia: Westminster Press, paperback), p. 76.

3. *Ibid.*, pp. 77–78.

4. John H. Schaar, "Reflection on Authority." *New American Review*, Vol. 8, 1970, pp. 75–77 and 78.

5. Interestingly enough, many of the more sophisticated business leaders are arguing that an effective executive is a man who is able to combine the other roles of leadership we have described above with competency in administrative tasks.

Chapter Six
CONCLUSION

In this book I have argued that to understand the
Church we must first recall our experience of church,
then investigate the New Testament to find out what
the kingdom is that Jesus came to preach, and finally determine the relationship between the kingdom and the
Church. The Church is an assembly of those who are committed to the kingdom, who work for its realization while
knowing that the kingdom comes in God's time not ours.
Through this kind of understanding we can approach the
theology of the Vatican Council and the leadership crisis
of the Church with a perspective which will at least point
directions for the future (though not necessarily solve all
our problems and difficulties) and give us confidence that
the Spirit is still at work in the Church.

This is, perhaps, the most appropriate note on which to
conclude. For it is through the Spirit that God works for
the Church; and it is through the gift of the Spirit that we
come to understand more deeply what the Church is. We
are more able to grasp implications that our predecessors
did not see concerning the Church's role in the world.

Hans Küng has beautifully described the Spirit's role in
the Church. Only when one believes that God's Spirit is
working in the Church, giving us a "recreated childhood,"
can we view with confidence, even joy, the never ending

transitional crises that seem to affect the Church. The Church is the temple of the Spirit, and it is ". . . the work and the tool, a sign and a witness of the Spirit of God which fills it. It is, to use the scriptural image, a temple, a building filled and reigned over by the Spirit: *a building of the Spirit.*"[1] But immediately our stubborn skepticism reasserts itself. St. Praxides and St. Ursula—a building of the Spirit? Great Heavens, they don't look that way! But we must remember that the scripture insists the Spirit works where he will and when he will, and that he can work with the most imperfect and fallible of human tools. We cannot, of course, rest content with the imperfection and the fallibility of the St. Ursulas and the St. Praxides; but neither can we deny that the Spirit is capable of working through them. Quite the contrary, it is a matter of faith for us that even in these very incomplete and inadequate Christian communities the Spirit is still present, taking possession of us, opening us to new things—to life and the future—giving us a new, recreated childhood.

Perhaps the most striking development in recent years of our insights into the nature of the Church is the recognition that, as Dean Colin Williams puts it, "the Church is also a servant of the secular society." Father Brown insists quite correctly that one cannot read this notion of service back into the words of the New Testament. But, on the other hand, to reflect on the meaning of service, to extend service to include that of the development of the whole world is a perfectly valid continuation of the message of Jesus. The Church is a city set on a hill, a light shining in the darkness; it is leaven in the dough, it is the salt of the earth. We understand more clearly today than in the past that one cannot distinguish between the work of creation and the work of redemption, that even making the world a more human place will not cause the coming of the kingdom, although it is an essential prerequisite for

the kingdom. It is, in any event, part of the charge that
Jesus has given to his followers: to act towards all one's
fellow men as one would toward him. Dean Williams
points out that in fulfillment of the servant ministry, the
Church has two roles to play:

> In its own internal life it practices the servant way in
> such a fashion that its community life becomes an illus-
> tration of the new way. "Bear one another's burdens and
> so fulfill the law of Christ." (Gal. 6:2.) Externally, within
> the structures of the world, the church is also called to
> take the servant presence of its Lord. This is made clear
> in the letter to the Ephesians. The first part of the letter
> tells how the life of Christ has removed the veil that had
> kept the secret of God's purpose for history hidden. In
> Christ, God has shown that it is his purpose to gather all
> things in heaven and earth alike into unity in Christ. The
> second part of the letter then spells out the practical
> meaning of this for the church . . . as a separate institu-
> tion. (Eph. ch. 4.) The quality of the life of the new com-
> munity must reveal the true nature of life in Christ. But
> that is followed in the subsequent chapters by a description
> of how this "walk in love" is to work its way out into the
> institutions of the world—into the family (ch. 5:22 ff.) and
> into master-slave relationships (ch. 6:5 ff.).[2]

Today, "walk in love" means a concern about race, pol-
lution, peace, population. It was not conceivable to Paul
when he wrote. But given Paul's view of things, it is by no
means an exaggeration to say that if he were alive today,
he would agree that concern about the social problems of
the world is completely in keeping with his message to the
early Christians.

Unless relationships in the Church radiate love, it will
not be a light set upon the mountaintop. As Colin Williams
says:

> . . . it [the Church] knows the world, hearing the claim
> that Christ has brought to the world a life of love that

carries with it the power to transform the ways of the world, will turn its eyes to the life of the community. There it should expect to see the evidence of that life: disciples who are "servants for Christ's sake" and a community where the new way is throwing light onto the dark spots of the world's trouble.[3]

But it is not enough that we love one another. Our love must flow out to the rest of the world if it is to take seriously our claim to be bringing Good News. The Church must be "leaven and salt to the world."

Leaven identifies itself with the lump, but in so doing it slowly changes the character of the whole lump. In like fashion the church is called to work within the world with the leaven of Christ's serving love, looking to the time when Christ's love will be all in all, and he will be known as the head of creation.

The church is called to work as salt within the institutions so that they can serve God's purpose by keeping order, peace, justice, health, and by using all their possibilities for enhancing human existence. By preserving institutions from decay they are enabled to fulfill their positive roles; by bringing out their true flavor it better enables them to satisfy the hungers and need of those they serve.[4]

There are obviously all kinds of complexities involved in the "salt" and "leaven" mission of the Church. My own inclination is to think that this does not mean that the Church as an institution should engage in direct political action nor that it should endorse one set of political solutions as being more desirable than others. I am inclined to think, rather, that the Church as an organization has a twofold role: it denounces unacceptable solutions to world problems (discrimination, racism, waste of the world's resources) and it urges its members to develop the competencies and skills and commitments necessary to transform the world. Far too many Christians at the present time equate moral enthusiasm with technical competency, sincerity and good will with practical know-how. I am not saying that vision, dedication, and zeal are irrelevant; quite the contrary, I do not believe that we can be salt or leaven to the world without these qualities. But neither do I believe they are a substitute for competency, skill, and the capacity to lead men by challenge rather than by denunciation. I am convinced that naive enthusiasm is both ineffective and short-range. Only commitment buttressed by competence will survive in the long-run.

But these questions, important though they are, must not be permitted to obscure the principal point of this concluding chapter: Only through the guidance of the Spirit who has brought us new life and new joy can we come to understand that Christians preach the gospel to the world not simply by word but by deed, by being a light on the mountaintop, salt of the earth and leaven in the dough. We cannot neglect our internal relationships, neither can we neglect our external responsibilities. For if we are only light we will not be heard; if we are only salt and leaven without light, the salt will have no savor and the leaven no strength.

It is absolutely essential, however, that as we play the role of leaven and salt, we understand what our motivation really is. It is frequently asked how Catholic involvement in social action is any different from anybody else's. The substance of the involvement may be no different at all. We have no monopoly on peace, justice, or the defence of natural resources. What ought to be different is our style and motivation. We ought to be more generous, more loving, more joyful, because we have a profound commitment to the Good News. The kingdom of God has come, the Really Real is Love, and in the long-run, the kingdom of justice and peace will triumph. If we lose this conviction in the midst of our feverish commitment of service to the world, then not merely do we cease to be followers of Jesus of Nazareth, but we cheat the world out of the vision that our commitment can offer.

One of the profound insights of the Vatican Council was that the God who created is the same God who redeems; that the pilgrimage of the human race toward fulfillment and the pilgrimage of God's people toward the parousia are, in the final analysis, the same procession. For the last two centuries this joint pilgrimage has paused at an oasis, a way-station called the modern world. Now the camp is breaking up. There is excitement, hustle and bustle, anticipation and fear. The tents are being taken down, baggage is being loaded onto the animals. One can even imagine John Wayne striding about announcing to all and sundry, "We're moving out! We're moving out!" Where do those of us who are part of the Church of Christ belong in this period of camp-breaking? Burrowing into the ground for safety? Hiding in our tents to avoid the shock of excitement in the camp? Standing about wringing our hands and issuing denunciations?

I think not. If the truth be told, we do not belong in the camp at all; we belong out in the desert, out with the scouts and the pioneers in the vanguard. We should be climbing the mountains to peer into the valleys beyond. Then, in our Joshua role, we should return to camp, say to our fellow pilgrims: "Do not be afraid to resume the pilgrimage. Do not be afraid to cross deserts and climb mountains, for there are many and splendid things in the country beyond. We know. We have been there already."

NOTES

1. Kung, *The Church,* p. 169.
2. Williams, *The Church,* pp. 89–90.
3. *Ibid.,* p. 141.
4. *Ibid.,* pp. 142 and 145.